Women Living
CONSCIOUSLY
BOOK II

Real Stories of Women
Living on Purpose,
with Passion, Empowered

Powerful You!
PUBLISHING
Sharing Wisdom ~ Shining Light

Women Living Consciously Book II
Real Stories of Women Living
on Purpose, with Passion, Empowered

Copyright © 2015

Cover Design by Jodie S. Penn
Editor: Sheri Horn Hasan

Published by: Powerful You! Inc. USA
www.powerfulyoupublishing.com

Library of Congress Control Number: 2014959370

Sue Urda and Kathy Fyler–First Edition

ISBN: 978-1-4951-3648-1
First Edition January 2015

Self Help / Women's Studies

Printed in the United States of America

Dedication

This book is dedicated women everywhere.
May you enjoy your journey of conscious living
and discover the beauty and truth of
your authentic self.

Table of Contents

Foreword

Be the Butterfly! This was the mantra for a series of workshops I led a couple years ago. The title and mantra came from the words of Mahatma Gandi, "You must be the change you want to see in the world."

In experiential art and mindfulness workshops, I had noticed how many people were fascinated by the butterfly and wanted to use the image in their artwork as a sacred symbol for the changes they were going through. We had discussed that the word, butterfly, in ancient Greek was Psyche and meant both butterfly and soul. So, this word and image of the butterfly had significance as a way of artfully representing their transformation.

From that, we adapted the Gandi saying and the love of butterflies to create a new mindful art workshop called BE the Butterfly! It was both fun and serious the "work" going on: identifying what changes were needed and wanted, declaring desires, developing action plans, practicing stillness, and appreciation for process.

Through breath, movement, mindfulness, sharing and creativity, the groups explored the creative chrysalis of their evolving lives. The workshop ended with them making a piece of artwork which revealed their metamorphosis and usually had a butterfly portrayed. Everyone always looked so pleased. The butterfly! The beautiful winged creature flying with new possibilities. It represented how they wanted to see themselves.

But then, I noticed something about the process—everyone wanted to be a butterfly. Mostly women participated in these workshops, and they clearly related to the beautiful images of the butterflies and the visions they had for their lives.

My observation and pondering led me to questions: *What if you are a caterpillar? What if you are the egg? The pupa? Was the goal only to be the butterfly?*

Humorously, people questioned my questions. Of course, the goal is to be the butterfly. Yet, my own observation of my life invited this questioning. My own transformation had occurred through a series of changes. I believed I had to experience each phase the way I did to truly appreciate the growth, and create an environment for continuing development.

I was not just one butterfly. I was a series of butterflies. I laid eggs...I munched on leaves...I spent time being broken down and rebuilt...I flew away and started again.

Living consciously is being fully awake and aware of the process in the midst of the outcomes. We may have goals to achieve and know what changes we want to see, but it seems it is how we embrace the process that can make all the difference.

To be a woman living consciously in our culture requires a depth of being. There is a seeking process which leads us to become aware of who we are and how we are made, and how this relates to who we are becoming. Sometimes a major crisis wakes us up, and we recognize we cannot and will not continue as we have. Sometimes this is sudden, and other times it is a slower process of awakening and realizing we need to make shifts.

Once we become aware and make the decision to live more deliberately, it activates our higher consciousness. We go through the seasons and cycles of our life with new perspective, recognizing the metamorphosis with sacred appreciation. We may not always understand what has happened to us and why, but the process of observing and discerning, leads us along a conscious path.

Some of us have had powerful and hurtful experiences. These happenings can leave us scarred and scared. Yet, notice, that the letters in the word *scared* are the same as *sacred*. As women living consciously, we have the opportunity to see in a way that encompasses a bigger picture with greater meaning and greater vision for how to move through the challenges and experiences.

Embracing sacred awareness allows a revealing and receiving...it empowers our vulnerability. Being vulnerable is frightening for many. It makes us think of weakness, yet, to be vulnerable is to be open and have an openness to process.

If the caterpillar refused to become the pupa, if it refused to go through the breaking down, mushy, mysterious phase, then there would be no butterfly.

Living consciously cultivates sacred awareness as we walk in our beauty, power and truth. Our experiences and our discernment illuminate what we truly desire. Living consciously, we "see" divine presence within and all around. This "seeing" becomes a knowing in which healing, wholeness, perfection and creativity are made manifest as we connect to a greater blueprint of who we truly are. As we connect, our lives shift on every level.

Our very cells vibrate and move to calibrate with this conscious awareness of cosmic divine design. Our souls come alive in this new, more whole and holistic way of being. Our hearts become the alchemic space for moving with greater grace, ease and passion for the life we are meant to be living.

In our everyday lives, to live consciously invites us to a discipline of attention and attending to details and tasks. How do we live as this conscious being? It is an integrated process involving body, mind and spirit.

Choosing how we live on every level enriches our evolution. What foods do we eat? How well do we detox? Do we exercise? Meditate? Do we practice gratitude? Have mindful awareness of our words and actions? Do we choose peace? Do we choose *love*?

The act of creating and acquiring beauty and inspiration in our lives and for our surroundings is a powerful way of creating a current of consciousness. Art, books, music, gardens, mindful cooking, etc. have tremendous value and inspire us as we grow and change.

At the core of living consciously, is the essence of knowing who we are, what we want, and that we have the power within to BE this and more. Our devotion to the process yields amazing possibilities and results. We travel through the fires and storms of life, refreshed by the cycles, creating newness from the fertile cast offs, and trusting that all is well.

Living consciously is a psycho-spiritual approach lived out through our physical experiences. We embody a sacred process, and as we choose to deeply love, respect and accept ourselves on every level, and in turn, we experience ecstatic transformation.

When we live with this as our core essence—when we authentically express our true selves—this becomes the change we need and the world needs. This presence inspires others to be in process as well.

In the pages of this book, we meet courageous women, who share their stories of becoming aware and living consciously. Their stories touch us heart and soul...inspiring...encouraging...illuminating ways of being. Their journeys create an awareness for the reader. We discover how to free ourselves and embrace new opportunities. We see we are not alone. On the contrary, we are all One. We can benefit as we share our stories. We are uplifted and emboldened to seize the process before us.

Women living consciously is a powerful antidote to much of what ails the world today. We need to be present to the process and walk powerfully along this path. Our self-discovery can be guided by the awareness that all of this hard work need not be so hard. We take ourselves far too seriously, are self-critical, and judge ourselves harshly. We must choose to move through these cycles with gentleness and love.

Does the caterpillar criticize the egg it once was for only being that egg? Or does the caterpillar appreciate the egg for being what it was, so it can now be at this stage. Does the butterfly criticize the caterpillar for spending much of its time crawling along eating leaves? Or does the butterfly appreciate that the caterpillar followed its divine design, gathering nourishment and nurturement for its next stage?

The creative chrysalis is powerful, and living consciously allows us to embrace and enjoy the growth.

Women living consciously creates and yields a powerful emergence of love and well-being which benefits all. With this powerful and positive state of being, it radiates outward touching and inspiring all persons to move through their metamorphosis. To be the butterfly is to appreciate the epiphany of process.

I am very grateful to be part of this wonderful book and to experience the wisdom of these women authors.The celebration of process and the triumph of spirit will engage the reader and inspire living consciously in ways which will help to transform and encourage all persons to cycle and soar.

Thank you.

Peace, Love & Blessings,

Reverend Robin V. Schwoyer
www.PinkHeartsWellness.com

Introduction

Waking up and living consciously is not something that you learn and then forget. Once you step into the realm of a more conscious existence, there's no turning back—it's as if a switch has been flipped, and you know it's only the beginning of the journey. As the title suggests, these women are *actively* engaged in the art of *living consciously*, and they are doing it right now.

Conscious living shows up in many different ways, and there's nothing typical about it.

For some of the authors in this book, it happened over time, through effort and attention. For others, it happened almost immediately due to an unexpected event or a 'rude awakening'. And for others still, there was a more subtle transformation that seeped in gently over many years and a multitude of experiences.

No matter the form or the time required for them to wake more fully into their lives, each of these women took the responsibility as her own—she took it to heart. They nurtured their discovery process and made sometimes painful decisions in order that they live with more feeling and truth. They stepped away from judgment and fear that they realized was often self-imposed. And all of them found comfort and even peace to know that they were not alone in the quest for the freedom that comes with living a more conscious life.

You are not alone either. As Robin says in the foreword, we are all ONE.

Two common threads woven through each story in this book are courage and faith: courage to look deeply into her own predicament, circumstances, and thought patterns, and faith to know she was the only one who held the power to effect change.

I want to help other women through my story... were the words I heard most often when I spoke with each of these authors. Choosing to bare their souls was not a selfish act, but one of compassion, empathy and honor. They each knew that their story may inspire, encourage, and assist the readers. They knew that they did not go through the tough and sometimes unbearable happenings only for themselves, but also to be of service in some way—often through the telling of her story.

As a student of both yoga and golf, I know that it is in the ongoing practice that my flexibility increases and my game improves. The more I engage and the more attention I give to each movement, pose, and stroke, the better I become and the more muscle memory I develop. Soon I know, the movements will be ingrained, they will become rote, and I'll experience more enjoyment and freedom in the process.

The same is true of living consciously—the more often we intentionally practice it with mindful attention, the more easily it will develop and the more naturally it will flow.

Open your mind and heart as you take in the words by these courageous and incredible women. Draw the lines that will inevitably connect you to the stories. Notice your heart space expanding, your empathy growing, and your own desire to wake more fully into your own conscious way of being.

Feel whatever feelings emerge and know that they are here for your highest and best good.

I am humbled by the strength and audacity of these women, and grateful that they have found their way together as co-authors in this book, so that you may take part in their journeys.

You are an extraordinary creature capable and deserving of great good. I invite you to step further on your own path of conscious living, now lighted by the words of these authors. And always remember to enjoy the process.

With great love and gratitude for you,

Sue Urda
www.sueurda.com

PART ONE

Conscious Well-Being

*"When a woman rises up in glory, her energy is magnetic
and her sense of possibility contagious."*
~ Marianne Williamson

My Seasons Of Transformation
Debra Wilber

The Fall Of Discontent

Life is good.

I'm enjoying a glass of wine and the breathtaking view of the Kuchumaa Mountains from the patio of my hacienda in Mexico's *Rancho La Puerta Spa* in late summer. I love *"The Ranch,"* which I discovered fourteen years ago–the peace it brings to my soul, the renewal it brings to my body, and the enlightenment it brings to my mind.

My buzzing BlackBerry interrupts my enjoyment of this little slice of paradise. Its insistent buzz won't be ignored. When I finally pick it up, I begin reading alarming messages from my staff about drastic changes at work.

Before I left for vacation, I was advised of potential changes and told not to worry–that everything would be fine. Now I'm shocked to learn that most of my colleagues are no longer with the company and that our department is being reorganized!

Oh my god, what if I don't have my job soon? I worry, as my anxiety level shoots into overdrive. Two of the things I value most–career and financial stability–are suddenly at risk! I've spent my entire career at this company and love it like a family. Most of my coworkers are friends; we work hard and play hard. We've done great things together, and I am proud of our achievements. Instantly, my world turns upside down.

Back to work–and reality–within a week, I try to figure out the next steps for myself and my staff. I'm told I can maintain my title and salary, and that there's a position for me in the new structure, but my trust in the organization is waning.

I try to move forward and ignore the fact that I am miserable. I begin to dread going to work and, after more than a few sleepless nights, realize it's time for me to move on—I've lost my spark, and somehow none of this matters to me anymore. Something inside is stirring and I know it's time for a change.

While I have no idea what my next step should be, I do know it's not looking for a new job! I create a financial plan for myself, which helps me remain sane. Worn out, I consider retirement. *Retire at forty-seven?* I ponder. While I'd always planned to retire early, this is sooner than expected. However, with nearly twenty-five years of service, it's an option.

Then one beautiful fall morning, with little contemplation and even less planning, I walk into my office and begin my retirement process. I'm scared—but it's the good kind of scared. The girl who always has a plan doesn't have one now, even though I know I'm starting the next phase of my journey.

The day before my last day at work I'm invited to a book signing in New York City. The author, Sue Frederick, is a renowned intuitive who just published a book on finding one's life purpose. I remember thinking *I'm happy—I'll be embarking on a new phase of my life in less than twenty-four hours,* but then the Salvation Army bell ringer on Fifth Avenue looks at me and says: "Smile, it can't be that bad!"

Aren't I smiling? I wonder.

A Girl With A Plan

From the time I'm thirteen I have a plan focused on success and financial stability. I grow up in a loving family with an abundance of support, hugs, and laughs, but not a lot of money, and often times are tough.

At thirteen I hear my parents despair over money. I remember that night still, lying in bed, listening to them discuss the prospect of losing our home—it's a dark moment! In that instant I make a commitment to myself: *I'll never let this happen to me!*

I *know* I'll attend college, even though I have no idea where the money will come from. There's never a discussion, I'm simply certain I'll go. I work many jobs—in fact, one summer my mother and I work five part time jobs! Tough times but fun, every semester I worry that I'll receive a phone call telling me I'll have to drop out.

Luckily, that call never comes and I graduate after four long years with a business degree in one of the worst economic periods. I find a job after six months, begin to earn a regular paycheck, and start spending money and accumulating debt. In the process, I forget my promise to myself.

Eventually I accumulate so much debt that I can't move out of my parents' house and, when I finally do, I boomerang back within a year. For a time, my love of *stuff* is more powerful than my desire for financial stability. My financial outlook seems bleak.

However, I'm out on my own and managing my money by the time I'm thirty. By thirty-five I've purchased my own home and lived in three states. I earn my Project Management Professional certification and executive status by forty, and by forty-five possess an M.B.A. in Finance and senior executive status. My career plans complete, I wonder what's left...

A New Year

Now forty-seven, I'm miserable and retired without a plan. I've lived my life up to this moment focused on career success and financial stability. I've accumulated material possessions and followed my plan but not my heart. I realize now it's time for my heart to catch up with my plan!

During the following year I experience the *fall of discontent,* the *winter of excess,* the *spring of discipline* and the *summer of fun.* My *fall of discontent* is painful fuel for my retirement. My *winter of excess* begins with Thanksgiving and proceeds through March. Since I don't have to get up and go to work, I jump from the rigors of the corporate treadmill to enjoying time as a couch potato. I eat too much, drink too much, and sleep too much. Then one day I wake up and my pants don't fit.

My *spring of discipline* includes diet and exercise. I start walking, which clears my head and allows me to focus on my heart. I begin to feel better physically, but emotionally am still confused. I *know* I have a greater purpose—I simply don't know what it is! I'm looking for the lightning bolt—the one that will strike me and tell me what to do.

I rewrite my resume and look for a job, though I know I don't want one. All my ideas of the past twenty-five years begin to come back to me—*I could open a restaurant, move to the beach, get another job!*

I'm offered jobs, but a new job will be more of the same and thinking about it makes me feel sick to my stomach. Still, I decide I'll do project management work as a volunteer and keep myself entertained. To help me figure things out, I hire a coach and—while working together that spring—we both know he isn't going to find me a job. However, he does give me a valuable gift—the space I need to grow and discover myself.

The *summer of fun* is my coach's idea after I bang my head against his desk chanting "why am I here and what's my purpose?" for the millionth time.

"When's the last time you took the summer off?" he asks softly.

I bolt upright, bewildered. "Take the summer off? Are you crazy? I'm trying to figure out my life's purpose! I have bills to pay!"

Eventually, though, I sit back down and listen to his advice. The last time I had a summer off it was 1976 and I was thirteen.

The Fall Of Discovery

When the student is ready, the teacher will appear. Sue Frederick's *I See Your Dream Job* ignites my transformation, though I'm not fully aware of this at the time. I read it a couple of times that year and its message resonates deeply. I follow Frederick on social media, and when she offers a free webinar near the end of my *summer of fun,* I sign up!

She speaks about intuition, birth paths, and purpose, and I love every minute! I feel my spark coming back! I'm ready to rely on intuition to guide my next step.

As my *summer of fun* ends and my *fall of discovery* begins, I sit on the patio of the same Mexican hacienda, enjoying the familiar view of the Kuchumaa mountains. Now I feel like I'm on the precipice of that mountain and there's something new on the horizon. *The Ranch* delivers the peace, renewal, and enlightenment I need as I continue my journey.

When I decided to take the summer off, I created a plan for the fall. I return from *The Ranch*, cancel the appointments with consulting companies and networking contacts I made as part of my plan. I know now I wasn't listening to my intuition before my *fall of discovery*. Instead, I lived still in my logical mind and listened only to my fear and not to my heart.

This fall I discover my intuition, which becomes my GPS, and I begin to live my life using this intuition as my guide. I research training. I don't create a list of pros and cons. I don't perform a cost benefit analysis. I don't create a plan. I locate a coach training program that feels right and sign up. I start to coach people—and in helping them find their purpose—I find mine!

A Girl Without A Plan

It turns out that the girl who always had a plan never really needed one to discover her purpose! Like Dorothy in *The Wizard of Oz*, I always had the capability to achieve my goals, but what I needed was to learn how to embrace the journey and listen to my intuition.

Now, at the age of forty-eight, eighteen months post-retirement in the *spring of achievement*, I arrive at my lifelong goal of owning a small business. My former self would never have taken the risk of leaving the job security of a regular paycheck to open a small business, let alone start a coaching practice!

The universe works in strange ways. Every moment from my *fall of discontent* to my *spring of achievement* happened by design to prepare me for the present. My journey with money taught me to trust that the universe will provide. My education and work experience equipped me with the practical tools needed to help others.

Most importantly, my heart and intuition—which serve now as my GPS—allowed me to stop planning and start living! And I found my calling: to help others discover their true purpose and achieve their goals through a heart-centered plan. Now I embrace all that this life brings and appreciate *all* my seasons of transformation.

ABOUT THE AUTHOR: Deb Wilber's coaching practice *Real Life Spark – Igniting the Next Generation of You!* is designed to inspire you to take small steps that lead to big changes in your life as you co-create a plan that makes your goals attainable. Deb's journey is one of small steps and giant leaps of faith—from her childhood dream of becoming an astronaut to the achievement of her goal of entrepreneurship. Dedicated to helping clients find their inner spark, Deb's authentic style—a blend of executive experience, intuitive knowledge, business education and coach training—complements her passion to inspire her clients.

Deb Wilber
Real Life Spark....Igniting the Next Generation of You!
deb@reallifespark.com
www.reallifespark.com
201-230-1255 (cell)

The Last Holdout

Marni Esposito

I've given the L-rd everything—my family, my money, my husband in full-time ministry—but the food, oh no, that's for me!

This is how the conversation sounds in my mind when I realize I'm saying and doing all the right things that a woman of faith and valor should. However, my relationship with G-d is covered with a layer—call it a wall—of resistance.

I've struggled with my weight my entire life. Thin as a kid, I come from a family with unhealthy habits and by the time I hit middle school/high school age, that's it—I use food as a comfort. Long story short, food becomes my drug of choice.

Later in life while in a high pressure job, the more stress I experience, the more I rely on food. At forty, I walk out of a six-figure job and gain a tremendous amount of weight, tipping the scale at 280 pounds. I catch a glimpse of myself from time to time and realize I have an "issue" with food, but don't take it all that seriously. After all, I don't have high blood pressure and I'm not diabetic—I'm living a relatively happy life.

Me, myself and I are coping quite well while holding together a life of holes filled with food. Like the mortar gluing together bricks that form the wall, food has become my comfort—the one barrier that holds me back from that which I'm truly called to be.

One day, before leaving on vacation with my family and close friends, I receive a notice from my airline about its updated policy on "oversized" passengers.

Am I an oversized passenger? I question, as I struggle silently with my health, my weight, and my emotions. But I move along as I always do and plan the vacation.

I step onto the plane, thinking about the size of my seat verses the size of—I'll just say it—my butt, and break out in a slow emotional sweat. The plane takes me onward and upward to my

Disney adventure with no room to spare in my seat. An adventure for sure—ultimately it's one that proves to change my life...

"It Does Not Do To Leave A Live Dragon Out Of Your Calculations, If You Live Near Him." ~ J.R.R. Tolkien

I walk around Disney in pain, but look forward to the roller coasters. Soon I forget about my plane ride and, as I approach a dragon-themed ride with my entire party, jump into a seat. The attendant tries to close the harness over my head without success.

"My lady, we have a special seat for large breasted dragons," he says politely. His humor helps, and my family and friends get on the ride without me as I wait in the gated area for the next "large" seat. After taking my reign in the seat of shame, I join them again and laugh it off. "Large breasted dragon" now becomes the theme of the vacation. We all have moments of clarity, and mine is very public. Fun on the outside, frustration and fear on the inside, eventually this moment becomes the lynchpin for change.

I return home sick, as is so often the case due to my declining health.

"Marni, I've been talking to you for some time now about addressing your weight." says my doctor after taking one look at me. Sheesh, and I haven't even disclosed my dragon adventure yet!

"Sign me up for your stupid plan," I cut him off before he can say another word, "I'm ready!" The shock on his face is comical, to say the least.

This is it, I've had my three strikes and now I'm out! Some people hear the still small voice of the L-rd, but I need a swift two-by-four upside the head! G-d has my attention now and I have no choice but to begin to listen.

Oh, but the journey—or should I say the agony?—of having to take each brick, one at time, and examine it, own the emotional turmoil, and do the real work, is one about which I'm not yet fully aware. Soon I learn my decision means I must be honest with myself and others, make some difficult choices, true sacrifices, and change the culture of my home life. Mostly, I must make myself a priority and take care of me first!

What I don't know is how this will soon become a lifelong pursuit, and that eventually I'll learn the truth behind what I've heard a thousand times: if you don't have your health you don't have anything!

"When The Prison Doors Are Opened, The Real Dragon Will Fly Out." ~ Ho Chi Minh

Immediately after my return from "dragon land" the high holidays arrive. A Messianic Jewish believer, I attend services with an openness I've never experienced before. To be honest, it feels more like a raw wound as I feel my guard wall—my last holdout—begin to crumble and be replaced by fear. Fear of failure—of disappointing G-d, disappointing myself, and of the painful exposure to change itself—weighs heavily on my heart.

There's an ancient Jewish prayer called the Al-Chet read during Yom Kippur. This prayer "confesses" a comprehensive list of sins. Suffice it to say that if a sin is not on this list, it does not exist. Not meant to be a punitive exercise, it's one of true reflection and introspective searching.

In all honesty I've read this prayer year after year, but this time I've already been hit upside the head with that two-by-four, and though my wounds are open my heart is ready to receive.

And there it is: "And for the sin which we have committed before You by eating and drinking..." What? When did someone slip that one in? In the name of all things holy I'd never read this before! Well I'd read it, but never received it.

Now let's be clear: food and drink are not sinful. But "gluttony?" That's a different story! At this point in my life I know that my relationship with food has become an idol—a wall between the relationship I could have with my creator, and with everyone and everything that surrounds me.

I use the abundance—or denial—of food as reward and punishment, and as comfort and discomfort. It's become my life's be all and end all. I'm living in extremes: all or nothing, yes or no, in or out, up or down, and this roller coaster of emotions, reliance, denials, and divisions make a prisoner of my soul.

A believer, I understand the "no sex, drugs, and rock and roll" euphemism for acceptable behavior. In many communities of faith, food has become an acceptable alternative to sin. It's social, legal, plentiful, and enjoyable; it brings us back to festival foods and family remembrance—so what's the problem?

I come to realize that most sin is on the inside undetectable to the outside world until we reveal it in some way. However, my weight is an external manifestation of my inward struggles that the whole world can see! Please don't misunderstand—I'm not saying that each and every pound I might need to lose is a sign of sin—but being trapped in a 280 pound body is not the temple in which my G-d intended me to live!

My body, my life, and my choices are living testimony to the power of the creator in my life each and every day. It becomes crystal clear to me during that Yom Kippur service—and for the sin which we have committed before You by eating and drinking—that my withholding in this one area in my life, this last surrender, this last holdout, is about to become the greatest struggle and ultimate liberator of my faith.

The Perfectionist Gene

With the help of my doctor, I make a plan. The first time I'm able to stick with something, I lose a significant amount of weight—100 pounds!—and start to refer friends and family to him.

"Marni, I'm a great doctor," he says one day, "but a lousy coach—you should become a coach!"

So I do, mostly as a hobby, and in July 2010 attend the Take Shape for Life national convention. This is it, I marvel, the mother ship! I've totally found my tribe! This is where I need to be and what I must do!

I become a certified health coach through their program, and almost four years later I've helped hundreds of clients lose weight and change their lives—and I've replaced my six-figure income!

I am in no uncertain terms telling you that I have this all tied up in a neat, tidy, and beautiful package. I've lost and gained and lost again a significant amount of weight since my "vacation epiphany." I know now that when I replace my relationship to G-d with food, it becomes a block and prevents my spiritual, physical, and mental success. I realize the ongoing battle for the rest of my life will be the surrendering of food before Him.

As a woman, I believe many of us have been cursed with a perfectionist gene. While some of us manage not to turn it on and accept right away that nothing and no one is perfect, I've spent my life living in extremes and striving for nothing short of perfection. When perfection seems unattainable, I succumb to the complete opposite and wallow in failure. If I believe I'll never be thin, then why try at all?

This robs me of the joy of the journey, and my accomplishments along the way. It's then I remind myself that G-d—and G-d alone—is perfect. He is perfect and I am not, however much I want to be...

Now I know I cannot fail unless I give up, and that I have access to the power of true love and acceptance. Grateful for each and every struggle, trial, sorry set back, and imperfection, they make me stronger and allow me to help others who are hurting. I believe all learning, gifts, talents, and any other granting from G-d, is not for me alone but to be shared with others. If I've struggled in this way then so have others, and I am compelled to support them and help.

In a world where we're taught to look out for number one and take care of ourselves first, I say yes, but only so we may serve one another. I want to share with every heart, each and every body of faith, and every soul that has ears to hear and eyes to see, that we are the only ones affected when we have a "last holdout."

ABOUT THE AUTHOR: Marni lives in Hamden CT with her amazing husband Tom and her children Sarah, Joshua, Jacob and mom Cynthia. Her home is filled with many furry friends Matzah & Gracie her yellow labs, Oliver the best cat ever, and rescue rabbits. Life gets busy and complicated but by faith her family moves forward. They might take steps back but what pulls them forward is serving others. Marni says and believes, *Have faith; do good in your life and you will do well. Never give up hope and ride the waves of your dreams like a dragon rides the wind.*

Marni Esposito
Certified Health Coach
livehealthynow@hotmail.com
www.YouCanLiveHealthyNow.tsfl.com
203-430-1009

Breaking The Chain
Harriet Linder

The snow is pretty high, much higher than my three-year-old toddling body. Bundled into a snowsuit, boots, mittens, scarf and hat, I hold my father's hand as we walk along the shoveled path in front of our apartment building. It snowed the night before and today is one of those cold, sunny, winter days.

My father chooses a good spot. We play in the snow and start to make a snowman. I like the feeling of having some attention paid to me, even though he doesn't say much or display any affection. I'm happy but shy with him, this man who is my father.

This is one of the few times he's made a point to spend time with me and I sense that he, too, is enjoying himself and having fun. I begin to feel good, wanted, accepted, liked—even loved!—as though I'm someone special to him. The afternoon passes enjoyably. We walk home together, up the stairs to our apartment on Sixty-Eighth Street.

My mother is there waiting for us, not with hot cocoa and marshmallows, but with loud, angry words and accusations. She's angry that my father spent time with me and carries on loudly and horribly.

My father does not respond. He disappears into the shadows. I'm left alone with my very angry, hostile mother. I try to ease next to her, to be comforted and held in her warm embrace, but she's silent, stoic, and steadfast in her resolve to shut me out.

I cry unabashedly, tears streaming down my face as I run repeatedly into her body, smashing into her folded arms, trying to get her to open them and hold me. But she remains cold and angry. There is no loving light in her eyes. I am lost, despairing, and alone—like my father—in the shadows, trying to disappear.

That is the first time—the first of many—that my mother shuts me out, simply stops speaking to me as if I'm not there. I never know when it will happen. I'm afraid to speak or be observed, afraid of being accused of some unacceptable behavior and then shunned.

My father is an inconsistent soul, not available for cuddling and snuggling. I find out many years later that he's an undiagnosed schizophrenic. I can't reach him and he doesn't know how to reach out to me. A lost child, despairing and lonely, I hide, lurking in the corners of my home to avoid my mother's wrath.

Sadness And Alienation

Life at home is sad and harsh. I'm not allowed out to play until my mother can think of no more chores to give me. She mocks me when she catches me laughing or happy about something.

"Oh, look at her, she's smiling," she'd say sarcastically.

Fast forward to age sixteen. I've just arrived home and am in my room. I hear my parents fighting—yet again. Suddenly I hear a loud cry from my father, a push, a shove, and the sound of heavy footsteps retreating backward. My mother crashes into my room, clutching the top of her head.

"Harriet, help me!" What I see causes me to blanch in horror. A gash on the top of her head—about an inch long and a quarter inch deep—oozes blood onto her scalp and into her hair.

"What happened?" I ask, in shock.

"Your father kisssssssed me," she replies in the deep cutting tone she uses often when referring to my father. It's always *my father*, not her husband, who does something to her. He'd cut her with a razor.

My heart and soul are shredded ragged with rage, horror, and despair. I know he's crazy, but she's blaming me—again—for what happened to her! Now I have to take care of her, tend to her wound, and not tell anyone....

The oppressiveness and unpredictability at home make me afraid to bring friends to my house. I know my father cares for me, but his irrational and violent behavior keeps me far away from him. I live inside a shell. The atmosphere in the house is oppressive.

My father dies of cancer at age sixty, when I'm nineteen. As my mother cries insatiably about how much she loved him, I feel a huge sense of relief. The weight of the world is off my shoulders. My crazy, sick father is gone. No need to walk on eggshells anymore.

But life goes on. The scars and trauma of my early life stay with me. My mother is easier to deal with now, although often cruel and heartless. She's out for herself and anything she can eke out of life.

Her daughter, as in the past, is meant to serve her. Although I have a life of my own I operate dysfunctionally—when I step outside I appear completely put together, but on the inside I feel I might crumple at any moment.

Unable to speak up and often anxious, I sabotage opportunities that come my way, not believing that people might actually think well of me. In college, when asked to pledge for an esteemed sorority, I turn them down. I try out for a dance part in a school production and am invited back, but never respond. *Do they really want me? How can they?*

Numb to feelings of acceptance, trust, and love, I spend my early life trying to be quiet, perfect, and unseen. When people reach out, I am dumbstruck.

Only One Mother

After college, I marry a loving young man but continue to be anxious and fearful. His loud, boisterous voice scares me. I carry anxiety and unhappiness about myself and my past into my new life.

His love for me is unrelenting. Despite my early years and the many hurts and traumas, my life with him is a good one and, thankfully, separate from my family of origin. As his career develops and grows, we have two beautiful daughters.

My mother passes suddenly. I cry at her funeral, realizing that everyone gets only one—mother, that is. We weren't close, but I know I was good to her and would have no regrets.

As my daughters grow up and I get older, I begin to experience health issues. A breast biopsy, polyps in my large intestine, and removal of an ovary predate my approaching menopause, during which I develop joint pain in my hands. Sometimes my fingers swell so that I cannot open a door or hold a glass.

Our twenty-fifth wedding anniversary approaches and our girls—now eleven and fifteen—present a surprise for us as part of the celebration in the form of a series of skits depicting their view of our marriage.

My husband laughs in amusement as I watch our daughters—each playing one of us—portray a woman, wife, and mother who is passive, unassertive, and acquiescent. Although they mean to be funny and entertaining, I feel hollow, numb, and deeply disturbed. *Who am I to my children?* I wonder. *Who am I to myself?*

I decide to find out. I begin to see a therapist. I commit myself to clearing out my past so I can finally free myself of the old "me" and begin anew. Concurrently, my health issues—including menopause, arthritis, and sinus infections—are becoming more of a nuisance. Doctors prove unable to help.

I begin also to see a homeopathist who helps me to peel away layers of emotional trauma in order to get to core physical issues. A few months into my treatments, the homeopathist gives me a CD entitled *Coping With Post Traumatic Stress Disorder* and asks me to listen to it once a day.

Why is she giving this to me? I wonder. *Isn't PTSD a disorder of returning war veterans—people who have been through severe emotional trauma? Wait a minute—can that be me, too?*

Yes, there were days growing up when I felt that hell had ascended into my childhood home. My parents, two badly traumatized children and refugees from Hitler's Europe, endured years of hatred and anti-Semitism while growing up. They suffered the loss of their families and unspeakable terror before finally coming to America and finding each other.

Needy, hurt, and angry, they were poorly qualified to marry but found common ground in their Jewish heritage and physical attractiveness.

Only when professionals begin to validate the severity of the abuse, neglect, and trauma I experienced in childhood—and I begin to share my story with close friends—does a slow, gradual awakening to the oppressiveness of my younger years occur.

Childhood had not been ideal, warm, or fuzzy. I cried when watching *Father Knows Best*, knowing that I was not anyone's "Princess" or "Kitten." I never realized my life—so much better than being starved, tortured, or murdered in a Nazi concentration camp—was so horrific!

The hard shell I created to protect myself begins to soften. As realization after realization allow me to shed more and more trauma, I begin to bloom and blossom. I become more assertive with my husband. At first, he doesn't know what hit him. I have to step away emotionally to change my behaviors, and then gradually return.

I attend school to become a physical therapist assistant (PTA) and then a personal trainer. I discover blood analysis and become a Certified Natural Health Coach. With each new step, life becomes richer and fuller.

I take better care of myself with diet and lifestyle changes, and my health improves. I embrace my husband—and he me—with newfound love and greater emotional and physical expression than before.

Last Mother's Day in Colorado with my two loving, strong, and beautiful daughters, I share a vision I had of my mother during a Reiki session a few weeks earlier. I tell them how I watched my heart open up and pour out like molten silver all the sadness I carried for her through the years.

I share also that my mother is ready now to take back the personal sadness and tragedies of her own early years and carry them herself. In death, my mother can now move on, as I have in life.

At dinner that night the girls give me a card. On the front it says: *If I Know What Love Is, It Is Because Of You.*

I have succeeded in breaking the chain and spared my daughters from this legacy. At peace, I can relax now.

ABOUT THE AUTHOR: After receiving a Masters in French and Education, Harriet began a second career later in life. She is a Licensed Physical Therapist Assistant, a Certified Personal Trainer and a Certified Natural Health Coach and Educator. She holds certificates in Applied Microscope Technology and Biological Flow Analysis. Harriet helps her clients achieve robust health and renewed vigor with her health coaching and training. With her microscope, Harriet explains to clients what living and dried blood may indicate and creates nutritional protocols, along with exercise and lifestyle changes, to improve clients health and vitality.

Harriet Linder
Better Living Wellness, LLC
www.BetterLivingWellness.com
Harriet@BetterLivingWellness.com
732-266-7299

My Divine Truth
Milada Sakic

What's happening to me? I wonder as my head pounds, my bladder burns, and pain throbs in my throat and chest. My mind seems immersed in an enormous foggy cloud, and my feet can't feel the ground beneath them.

"Do I have some terrible disease?" I ask my husband Almir, terrified. "Or am I going insane? Or both?"

"Just rest now, my love" says Almir, much worry in his eyes.

Bedridden now for four days—my first sick days in fifteen years—I wonder: *can I give myself permission to get sick, rather than pushing through as I usually do?*

It's May 2012, but feels like a déja vu of my burnout experience ten years earlier when I developed similar strange symptoms.

"We have to do more tests, but are you feeling ok otherwise?" the doctor asked me in 2002.

Sure, I feel wonderful otherwise, except for a high intolerance to fluorescent light, noise, and certain vibrations audible only to me! I can't bear loud music or voices, and I wonder how dolphins and whales must feel—surrounded by all the sonar noise in the ocean. It's awful, and there's nowhere to escape this world of noise!

Try saying *that* to your family doctor!

Stress exhaustion was the doctor's verdict then. Of course, I had an astrological explanation: Pisces on the cusp of the 6th house of dis-ease, daily routine, and work environment, which can manifest as energies and vibrations related to environmental sensitivities. No one would understand these strange unexplained sensations of sensitivity unless they were also born an intuitive empath like me.

I wondered if a few weeks of vacation might fix it, but ended up quitting my job instead.

I'd been seriously overworked, putting in twelve hours a day, six days per week as an order management coordinator for a small company. Still, my pragmatically trained rational mind continued searching frantically for a physical explanation for months and years to come.

Now, however, my health crisis manifests as a complete immune system shutdown. Overworked yet again, as a nine-to-five executive level human resources professional in Toronto, I'd added a part-time weekend and evening astrological consulting practice, teaching astrology, and volunteering at a local astrology association.

In this vulnerable moment of awakening and clarity in 2012, I sit sobbing on the toilet seat in the small en suite bathroom of our condo as Almir holds my hands and asks if he needs to call 911.

The Warrior

Born with my umbilical cord wrapped around my neck, I'm saved by an emergency C-section. My mother always points to something blue to illustrate the color of my skin at birth, when I almost suffocated.

My astrological Sun—at 23 degrees 21 minutes of Taurus—aligns with the fixed star Algol, associated with experiences of danger to the neck.

The eldest of three children, I become hyper-vigilant by the time I'm ten. Throughout childhood my father is severely addicted to alcohol, and for as long as I can remember there's no peace to be found in our household. I don't want to miss a moment of my parents' arguing, and choose to stay by my mom's side—as if my presence there will help keep her safe. It doesn't.

Sometimes I hide in the bathroom to escape the incessant arguments, accusations, threats, hostility, and violence that plague our family daily. I feel so helpless, yet so defiant at the same time.

I experience rare moments of peace while writing poetry or taking the bus to school. This is also when I communicate with my guides—mostly telepathically—and ask when the insanity of this life will stop, and if we'll ever be safe in our own home.

Everything is all right and will be all right very soon, I hear, and instantaneously I calm down. This voice, or inner knowing, is never short of words to offer, and I don't doubt for a moment that God exists. *If my connection with God and guardian angels is real, then God surely hears my daily pleas for the safety and the wellbeing of me and my family*, I reason.

The potential to hear and communicate with this wiser inner voice nevertheless increases my uncertainty, mostly because it always sounds to me like it says simply what I want to hear. When nothing changes for the better and the situation becomes only progressively worse, at first I conclude: *God must be too busy to help me!*

Although I feel wise, strong, and ok deep within, keep the best grades in school, and win numerous literary awards, at the same time I'm profoundly helpless to protect my mom, stop my dad, protect my younger siblings, heal my family, and affect positive change. Externally I feel so powerless—as if thrown into a dark deserted abysmal hellish pit, or purgatory.

Eventually I decide I'm simply imagining being guided and protected, and that I must be making up this inner voice, which ultimately hampers my ability to understand its true purpose.

I start tuning out what I hear internally and, by my teen years, focus more on developing my technical and analytical skills.

I convince myself that I deserve this pandemonium in some karmic way, and that I'm meant to be a fighter, protector, and survivor. Thrown into the middle of all this to practice my fearlessness, I shut down this connection with my higher self and lose touch with my divine truth.

One Hundred Years Of Pain

Unsure if I need a doctor, a saviour, or simply my soul to come through, I continue to cry my eyes and heart out, a worried Almir beside me. I don't know in this moment if my soul wants to die, or if part of me is simply dying off. Sleep-deprived, I'm finally brought to my knees, ready to surrender to my soul—the part of me that refuses to accept a logical solution to every problem.

All of a sudden—as I'm relinquishing the pieces of my disowned or disallowed fragmented self—I feel an *entity* leave my body. For a few moments that feel like an eternity I struggle to gasp for air. It's as if I'm experiencing a severe allergic reaction and someone has injected anesthesia into my throat, which feels frozen and constricted at the same time.

Suddenly, it's like an invisible hand releases my neck, which at this point feels so narrow.

Through my haze of sobs, I hear Almir repeat, as if from a faraway distance: "Milada, dear, I am here...I love you...I love you! I am here with you!"

In this moment, these become the most healing words I've ever heard in my entire life! A surge of unconditional love and forgiveness overtake me, and envelop my soul—as if soothed in the arms of the gentlest and most gracious of angels.

Just be...just be love...be unconditional love, reveals my higher self in this moment of peace-full realization. Finally, now my inner critic approves! Why do I need to attract a crisis to hear, honor, and act on my inner wisdom—the voice of my soul over that of my mind? I realize now I've approved all along, but simply chosen to override and disregard my soul's voice previously.

Be forgiving to yourself as you are to others, I hear. *Do not try to be, do not vow and promise to be, do not struggle to be...perfect. Offer that which you are willing to contribute and share, that which you have found within in the most joyous of ways. Your mind is powerful, but your soul is wiser. By choosing wellbeing first, you align with your soul and ask your mind to be in service of your soul...*

I fall on the bed, heavy with a relief worth one hundred years of pain—perhaps even one thousand years of ancestral trauma and emotional baggage—and sleep firmly for the next few hours as Almir lies beside me quietly. At last I've found peace!

My Conscious Journey

What I find out from this experience is that a built-in alarm system goes off if I'm not completely sharing or speaking my truth, but rather suffocating it inside. Its purpose? Not to harm me, but to protect me! What a revelation! I'm so grateful and humbled!

Activated deep within my soul by two powerful eclipses in May 2013, I remember suddenly and very intensely craving inner peace. Sixteen years after my diligent hardworking journey through corporate Canada where I worked my way up from entry level to executive, I'm ready now for the next step of my conscious journey!

After months of careful deliberation and the heart-wrenching, painstaking analyzing of timing and responsibility, duty and destiny, I finally—cautiously but resolutely—approach my employer of twelve years about scaling down my work week from five days to four.

While this represents a gradual transition, I don't yet see exactly how I'll segue from here to there in its entirety. However, I'm determinedly ready and intuitively guided!

I'll never forget the day I decide to finally *ask* and to be completely open to *receiving*. This is because I know that the dose of *quantum* faith I must gather to lead to that electrifying moment of *asking* is going to powerfully activate a new, exhilarating, and very liberating phase of my life. A phase in which I'll choose wellbeing and wholeness first, finally embrace my highest potential, and step fully into my purpose to help others achieve the same!

What this new phase is going to be all about I'm not completely certain. However, I feel my inner faith expand peacefully, deliciously, fulfilling-ly, from my heart center to my crown chakra and back, throughout my whole body.

Despite trepidation, no fear or uncertainty is present—only butterflies in my stomach coupled with a sense of unhurried urgency, announcing that something beautiful and magical is going to happen. Something I'm going to have to hold my breath for, or better yet *breathe through*, and then open up fully to receive.

Since discovering the powerful wisdom of communicating with our divine guidance through our Akashic Record, I've had several massive mindset shifts. Yet my journey of transformation began years ago—perhaps even lifetimes ago—with every struggle, every battle, every success, every lesson, every victory, every divine soulful step essential in guiding me purposefully and unmistakably to this very moment of inner freedom and wholeness.

I realize now that my inner guidance—never short of words to offer—is an infinite stream of all-present wisdom that loves me to bits and is never separate from me! It's *not* my imagination. Instead, it's the integral part of me that's all-knowing and infinite—*my divine truth*—from which I receive an abundance of messages that resonate with pure joy and love!

ABOUT THE AUTHOR: Milada Sakic, author of the upcoming book *Wellbeing, Wisdom, and Wealth - Healing Keys to Conscious Living,* is a business coach and a highly sought-after transformational teacher, speaker, healer, and astrologer. She helps highly-conscious women and aspiring entrepreneurs fully align with their purpose, clear their money blocks, and choose the best timing to launch their lucrative ventures in order to create a thriving life and business they love. Milada has turned her passion for astrology and soul-level healing into a flourishing full-time healing and coaching business, within just one year of letting go of her corporate executive role as an HR Professional.

Milada Sakic
www.miladasakic.com
milada@miladasakic.com
www.facebook.com/miladasakic

Journey From
The Mind To The Heart
Jean Callaway

Violent physical, emotional, and sexual abuse invade my formative and teen years, and the men in my life—at last count at least eight of them—have their way with me, sometimes two at a time. Often bound and gagged, my life is threatened if I make a sound or speak of the abuse.

Instinctively, I shelve most memories somewhere outside myself and unconsciously disassociate from these experiences. Possessing no conscious memory of the abuse until much later on, I sleepwalk through life.

Diagnosed with a host of mental disorders, including post traumatic stress disorder (PTSD), dissociative disorder, depression, and limited cognitive ability, my daily survival kit includes a multitude of anti-depressants, pain killers, anti-anxiety pills, and other medications to help me sleep.

However, according to the "standards" set by society, I am successful. From the outside looking in, I lead a good "upper-middle class" life. Gainfully employed, a nice suburban home, the perfect family, and an above average family income, I'm a success—at least as defined by the rules, beliefs, and societal standards imposed upon me which I adopt and make my own, no questions asked!

The real truth is that I've never given much thought to anything of any significance at all. Always too busy taking care of everyone else's needs, I try desperately to live up to the standards of how the *perfect* wife, mother, sister, daughter, friend, and employee should look, act, dress, speak, think, feel, and be.

Oblivious to the obvious signs that something is amiss, all I do is step on the treadmill of life each morning and hit start. Unconsciously operating in survival mode, I possess only two robotic speeds—faster and stop. I experience my life as a never ending "to-do" list as I wander aimlessly with no specific purpose or reason for my existence.

The words *spirit, spirituality,* and *self* are not part of my vocabulary or conscious experience of life. Energy is simply something that powers my appliances. I can't even begin to conceptualize words like *conscious* or *consciousness;* there isn't room in my world for such *fluff.*

The *good life* as I know it comes crumbling down in March 2000 when my eldest sister dies. The shock of her sudden death pulls me deeper into an abyss of numbness and dissociation, seemingly a better place than having to face my reality and risk being sucked into the swirling pool of blackness I've cleverly avoided for so long for fear I might never return.

Years of living this way take their toll and wreak havoc with both my body and my mental/emotional well-being. One might think the diagnosis of elevated blood pressure and cholesterol, severe migraines, gastrointestinal problems so intense I vomit on a moment's notice—and a body wracked with pain—might have gotten my attention. Alive on the outside, I'm dying a slow and painful death on the inside and never even realize it.

The Awakening

The final blow is the diagnosis of brain and spinal cord tumours a mere five days after my mother's burial. I'd finished surgery, radiation, and chemotherapy treatment for breast cancer eleven months prior and—other than the remembering of a small inner voice that said *no way, you're not going to get me!*—the breast cancer diagnosis barely fazes me.

Now, deafened by the terror engulfing my body, the words "paralysis" and "possible death" are the only ones I hear as the neurosurgeon advises me of potential outcomes of emergency spinal cord surgery, which I require. That does it. I'm awake now—at least to the fact that I'm petrified and once again fighting for my very life!

The following morning, as I reflect on the state of my life—totally asleep, no connection to myself or spirituality—I'm struck with a profound personal awareness that I can't ignore: *I'm living my mother's life!* Her life, like mine, was a series of debilitating illnesses, isolation, and depression. Out of my mouth come the words "enough already—no more! This is not how life is supposed to be! This is my mother's life and I'm not living it!" I do not question the origin of these words; they burst out of me with a force much larger than life and literally place me on a new path.

Totally oblivious to the existence of alternative healing modalities, or the universe, or the law of distraction—as I refer to the life I once lived—a series of synchronistic events lead me to a local organization offering a two-day program on the application of the principles of quantum biology to human behavior.

In the blink of an eye at this weekend retreat I experience an instant awakening, and from that moment I'm picked up and placed on a new path and never look back. Eager to dip my toes into all this new world has to offer, I begin to question every single thing I've ever been taught—specifically related to dis-ease, consciousness, and what I've come to believe about who I am and the world around me.

This perspective so enlightens my mind that it's quiet for the first time in my life. Gone are the conversations with myself about what's right, wrong, good, bad—and my always judging, feeling judged, and obsessively trying to figure things out. Every cell in my being knows truth is being spoken as I'm introduced to a totally new life paradigm, which offers—among many other things—a fresh and empowering perspective on the roots of dis-ease.

Four days after the completion of a week long retreat—as I lay on the floor unable to walk with electric shocks shooting through my brain—I realize I've forgotten to take two of my anti-depressants. In that moment, I decide there's no way I'm ever again putting anything in my body that inhibits my ability to feel—no matter what!—and to ride this wave. The intense withdrawal lasts approximately eight days and within months I let go of all my other medications.

I withdraw from the life I once lived, defer the emergency surgery, and begin a journey to heal the spinal cord tumour naturally. On a much deeper level—and out of my conscious awareness at the time—I realize I've spent my entire life running, doing my best to suppress the experiences of my past.

Now ready to face the demons which torment me, I do not have far to go. The journey takes me into the deepest, darkest crevices of my body and conscious/subconscious minds. It's here I discover the forgotten memories of a childhood that robbed me of my consciousness and left me living life in a state of shock.

As I learn to shed the pain, grief, sadness, guilt, fear, rage, and self-limiting beliefs that ravish my body, mind, and spirit, I bear witness to the most incredible metamorphosis within and my physical and mental/emotional well-being begin to improve.

Yet it seems the more attention I give to healing my spinal cord tumour, the larger it becomes. Despite the huge amount of energy devoted to thoughts like I've tried my best and done everything possible to heal the tumour, it's bigger than when I started. What does one do when one does everything possible and still can't get it right?

Three years pass and my neurosurgeon strongly encourages me to have the surgery *now,* as the tumour is at the point of causing irreversible damage. Life in a wheel chair—dependent upon others to fulfill my every need—does not appeal to me, and I schedule the surgery knowing it will somehow bring closure to this chapter of my life and lead me in an entirely new direction.

"No Problem Can Be Solved From The Same Level Of Consciousness That Created It." ~ Albert Einstein

And so it does. Even though my mission is no longer to heal a spinal cord tumour, a powerful inner force propels me forward. Driven by a remembrance of curiosity and a deep inner knowing that anything is possible, I become deeply committed to my own evolution, personal healing, and truth. I go into semi-seclusion, studying and applying many alternative healing modalities including cellular and mind/body healing, energy medicine, consciousness, spiritual awakening, enlightenment, and more. At some point I decide to let go of the notion that there's a brain tumour, and stop seeing the neurosurgeon monitoring it.

Since my primary coping strategy is dissociation, this journey demands that I be willing to come in to my body. What a trip! Unbeknownst to me, as the truth of what I carry in this body reveals itself, there isn't one part of me that wants to be here! Over time, and after meeting and releasing even deeper layers of despair, hatred, panic, anger, guilt, frustration, grief, and rage, I come to understand that these emotions are not me at all. Rather, they are but memories of heightened emotions lodged in my cells from my childhood experiences.

As the shock begins to unravel itself, I start to understand I'm highly empathic and feel everything—yours, mine, and the planet's—all of it! Through a vision I learn how surrounding energy/consciousness moves and expresses uniquely through everyone and really come to understand, I am not this body—not the repressed energy, emotion, feelings, dis-comfort, and dis-ease which move through it.

This leads to another declaration: "Only me in this body!" which spawns a whole new question: Who am I anyway? Who is this me I demand be in this body? If this that I am is consciousness, what, then, is consciousness?

For the longest time this one puzzles me, as it seems as though consciousness is something outside of myself. Merriam Webster Dictionary defines it as the quality or state of being aware, especially of something within oneself.

I delve deeper and although I've heard it many times in many of the teachings, as I begin to heal my life, and let go of the trauma, projections, programming, rules, beliefs, and conditionings which were never mine in the first place, I activate my body's innate ability to heal and regenerate. I give myself permission to be authentically real no matter what the situation. I begin to love, honor, and respect myself and all life unconditionally, and to know that nothing "out there" has any power over me. The outer is a reflection of the inner.

Eventually, the light goes on and I really get it–I am the consciousness that is here always! With higher consciousness comes an inner power and the confidence, courage, strength, and resilience to make different choices; the power to consciously create a more meaningful, enjoyable experience of life. What started as a quest to heal a brain and spinal cord tumour led me on a fascinating and transformational journey of healing, self discovery, higher consciousness, energy, and–ultimately–the longest journey of them all: the journey from the mind to the heart.

ABOUT THE AUTHOR: An accomplished spiritual health and wellness coach, teacher, healer, intuitive, and guide, Jean's very presence becomes a living, breathing transmission of healing consciousness which transforms lives. Jean's quest to heal a brain and spinal cord tumor led to an intense and fascinating healing journey where self mastery, autonomy, rejuvenation, regeneration, and higher consciousness all became possible. Able to go beyond single healing techniques, Jean is one of those rare exceptional people who efficiently combines multiple techniques to help others heal. Generous, caring, and kind, Jean works with those who want more of what's possible–physically, emotionally, and spiritually.

Jean Callaway
jeancallaway@bell.net
613-295-2756

Reclaiming My Spirit
Barbara M. Schultz

My jaw drops and I scream in horror as I see Sarge, my elderly rooster, hanging upside down lifelessly by his talons from the chain link fence. His feathers soaked through, he'd apparently gotten caught earlier while leaping to fight. Now sunset, I've returned to the barn unusually late as torrential rain had imprisoned me indoors since morning.

Chilled to the bone, Sarge's head appears a mass of blood, his eyes indiscernible. The other fowl had pecked him mercilessly, taking advantage of his vulnerable position, as happens often to weakened animals—especially at the sight or smell of blood.

"I'm so sorry Sarge," I whisper as I untangle his talons quickly from the fence and hold him tight. Always a take-charge mighty leader, yet gentle and respectful around humans, I love Sarge and will do whatever it takes to save him—if he's still alive.

I feel him inhale and run hopefully to the well pump to rinse away the blood. I can't tell if his eyes are still intact.

Little do I know how my life's circumstances will soon mirror Sarge's...

In The Beginning

I attend church faithfully every Sunday from an early age, and my spirituality springs forth like a fountain from the depth of my soul. I pray at the church across from my high school before class. God is important to me.

Early childhood recollections grip my psyche with terror. At a young age I become hyper-vigilant and, like a cat trapped in a roomful of rocking chairs, stay small, still and silent, and pray to protect myself. Keeping super busy diverts my mind from terrifying memories but anesthetizes my fragmented soul to the wisdom of the present moment.

I marry at nineteen, only months before graduation from community college. I pass my registered nursing boards and birth four kids within a five year span by age twenty-seven. We move several times, all while I work various shifts as a nurse and attend graduate school two hours away. When you are asleep at the helm of your life and living unconsciously, life becomes a bull to be grabbed by the horns.

Not the gateway to solace for which I long, my marriage becomes a chess game of control and abuse. Dutifully, I secure my master's degree in nurse-midwifery and move kids and pets cross country for a job in an underserved area of Chicago. This last straw of stress collapses my marriage and my three daughters and I return to Rhode Island, leaving my ex and son in Illinois.

A couple of years pass and I reach for the golden ring again as the obvious answer to the peace and respite I crave. I remarry and give birth to my son at forty-five, months before my youngest daughter turns nineteen.

History repeats itself for those of us who don't learn our lessons from life's lumps and bumps, and this marriage turns out to be more of the same as the last. It's clear I haven't yet done the inner work.

To fill the emotional void and heart-wrenching loneliness of my marriage, and seduced by my dream to create a farm, I busy mind and body accumulating and tending animals who become the salve for my wound of unrealized expectations.

A few marriage counselors later, the decision to separate from my husband brings new challenges as I am forced to relocate my farm. Getting really good at this well-ingrained limiting pattern— moving and staying very busy—I replay it again as the default solution.

Moving On

On moving day—two days after Christmas and less than one month after starting a new full time job—friends and family arrive in droves to help. Furniture, clothing, feed, hay, supplies, and animals— including twenty or so goats, thirty-plus chickens, roosters, two big dogs, and a pair of cats—are relocated as if by magic. My farm now graces a small rental property in a neighboring town.

The universe aligns with my soul to propel me on my journey as if to say *let go of the oars and see how easily your life can flow downstream.* Ah, synchronicity...

Two weeks after settling in, I receive an urgent call at work from my brother.

"Mom called nine-one-one screaming in pain!" he reports. "The ambulance is heading to Memorial Hospital now—I'll meet you there!"

"Your mom has suffered several strokes," the doctor informs us. Though unresponsive, Mom nevertheless screams in pain intermittently over the next seven days. The nurse in the family and the health care proxy, I process decisions such as "do we amputate her leg?" and "do we remove the respirator?" with my siblings until Mom passes. I never really get to say good-bye. Ironic how the turmoil within one's thoughts often plays out as drama in real life.

Humpty-Dumpty

Fast forward to spring later this year. The rental house must be sold but is out of my price range. Another move, and my farm winds up two miles down the road in a foreclosed "fixer-upper" which only my wistful eye views as a diamond in the rough.

Naively, I trust the contractors to complete necessary renovations as promised. I keep busy, of course, racing through each day working as a nurse—and through dawns, dusks, and weekends as a single mom and farmer. I milk goats, gather eggs, fetch hay, haul grain, strip the barn, administer shots, clip toenails, make cheese and yogurt, and cook, clean, and do laundry. I have little time for friends and family.

My partially renovated house floods repeatedly. Unsupervised contractors, landscapers, and fence installers perform unsatisfactory work. I come home one night to find a fluorescent orange *Stop Work* sticker on my garage window—slapped there by the town because renovations haven't been completed according to code.

Too nice, too trusting, I give my power away...until I hit the inevitable wall...

One stifling August day, I jump at the chance to purchase hardwood tree stumps at a bargain price. I manage to hook up the horse trailer to the truck, pull it from the pasture, and inflate the tires. After several trips with my rig and lots of tugging and lifting to load and unload—sweat pours down my face, but I'm now the proud owner of a backyard full of wood to heat my home for the winter.

Just one small detail: all this wood needs to be split and stacked! Even with my gas-powered splitter, this will require both time and muscle. Summoning all my strength and stamina, I hoist stump after stump onto the splitter. I push beyond exhaustion, ignore the searing pain in my neck and arm, and convince myself it's something a hot bath will surely fix.

In the process, I suffer irreparable damage to my cervical spine that results in pain and neuralgia in my right arm. Unable to continue work as a hospice nurse who cares for sick and dying patients in their homes—which requires many miles of driving, climbing numerous flights of stairs with supplies, and heavy lifting— I have insufficient means to support my family and farm.

Plus, now I must hire extra help to run the farm. Doctors, physical therapists, and my chiropractor can't put this Humpty-Dumpty back together again. Like Sarge, bloodied and blinded in the fight, I'm without strength or stamina to continue. Suspended upside down by invisible talons, I hang helplessly in the balance with no choice but to surrender to a force larger than myself.

Restoration Of Spirit

Sarge can barely stand. A trophy bird despite his age, he proudly sported a colorful mix of forest green, cream, orange, and gold feathers that taper into a long plume of deep green. But no longer...

I carry my beloved rooster inside the barn to the kidding pen, a small fenced area for birthing goats warmed with a heat lamp that clips to the chain link. I know he'll be safe here, yet not totally isolated from the others, which would increase his stress. One of the brown hens from Sarge's harem takes her place loyally at his side in the kidding pen, providing companionship and support.

Weeks pass and Sarge regains his sight and strength, but not his rooster-ness. I let him out with the flock daily, only to watch him cower, limp along the fence, and hide. I carry him in at night to ensure he gets his share of grain and cracked corn. I wonder if nursing him back to physical health is the right choice. Losing hope, I coach, pray, and sing to him. How does one restore another's spirit?

One by one, members of Sarge's harem of hens join him in the kidding area. Finally the day comes when Sarge stands his ground in the barnyard. I watch his neck feathers splay out like a lion's mane. I wince as he fights; my heart leaps with every kick and twist I witness. I realize I have no control over the outcome and shouldn't intervene. Miraculously, Sarge wins this fight and secures his place as a flock leader!

I feel a palpable shift in the barnyard dynamics that day. The animals shuffle into a new pecking order, existing in a different reality now—one seemingly without grudges or complaints about unfair treatment.

Now able to rest and rekindle my spirit, I begin to realize how all my life I've been running on a treadmill to nowhere, trying to overtake my illusion of *not-enoughness*. All the while, I've hungered for something more because the deeper spiritual part of me wasn't being fed—until the universe helped me out.

Privileged in my work as a nurse-midwife and hospice nurse to experience the cycle of birth and death, I see now how I've been hanging in the balance between two worlds: the world of scarcity I'd experienced through my limiting beliefs versus the abundant world that knows no limits. Although I heard my soul beckoning me as a spiritual teacher, I kept myself habitually too busy and distracted to heed that call.

My struggles are the stepping-stones to my divine path, and I surrender to the rooster fight that is my life. From that place of letting go, and the steadfast love of those who stand beside me, my life becomes simple.

Through my work now as a transformational mentor, I take the hand of those anxious and depressed from life's challenges and help them step out in the world in a new way. Like Sarge, who eventually rallied through the courage gained from those who stood by him until he got on his feet again to fight and *win*, I've found the courage to birth a new life of happiness and abundance. Like Sarge, I'm reclaiming my spirit through the power of love.

ABOUT THE AUTHOR: Barbara Schultz, RN, CNM is a spiritual health and wellness expert and CEO of The Soul Midwife. Through her work as a transformational mentor and intuitive healer, Barbara coaches women who are anxious, depressed and feeling stuck in their stressful lives. Barbara helps these women transform anxiety into empowerment to create a life they love to live! An RN for many years, Barbara earned her MSN in Nurse-Midwifery from Yale University in 1992. In addition, she is Certified as a Reiki Master, Akashic Record Practitioner, and is skilled in a variety of alternative therapies.

Barbara Schultz, RN, CNM
www.thesoulmidwife.com
Barbara@thesoulmidwife.com
www.facebook.com/thesoulmidwife

Chemical Free From A To Z

Dale Schock

Oh my God, I can't breathe–am I having a heart attack? There's pressure on my chest, my heart's racing, and everything around me looks foggy. Sick to my stomach and dizzy, I'm also sweating profusely.

I'm terrified! Only twenty-four years old and these strange symptoms come upon me when I'm driving my children home from a routine doctor visit.

Subsequently I find out that I experienced an anxiety attack. Soon, I begin feeling anxious and fearful more frequently, particularly when leaving my house. The only place I feel truly safe is in my own home.

Eventually going out is not even an option for me and, as the years go by, my anxiety attacks increase. I begin to make excuses to explain why I don't attend my children's school functions, visit with friends and family, or go grocery shopping,

The truth is that I've become housebound, and the doctor diagnoses me as agoraphobic!

Five years after my agoraphobia diagnosis–essentially a fear of being in open or public places–I'm basically a hermit. Until...I decide to take back my life! With the help of family and friends, I'm able to overcome my anxiety, and slowly I rejoin the living. What a relief!

Finally, just as I seem to have gotten back to normal, I begin to experience pain in my abdomen and bleed so heavily each month that I'm stuck in my house for a week. When the pain gets so bad in the middle of each month that all I do is lie in my bed and cry, I decide it's time to visit the doctor.

Diagnosed with ovarian cysts and fibroid tumors, the cysts are so large the doctor is afraid they may be cancerous. I'm told I need a hysterectomy. My scheduled surgery that's supposed to take two hours lasts for five. I find out later that not only do I have huge tumors and cysts, but also endometriosis, which complicated my surgery.

Recovery from the hysterectomy is difficult. By now I'm forty and my hormones, or lack thereof, wreak havoc on my body and my emotions. Prescribed hormone therapy simply doesn't work; I stop taking it and hope for the best.

The Common Denominator

A year after my hysterectomy I start to notice rashes all over my body. No matter what I do, they won't go away! Within months my body is one giant oozing, itching, painful rash! Unable to tolerate even the most comfortable clothing, or lie down in bed, my doctor diagnoses me with *contact dermatitis* and prescribes a steroid and an antibiotic.

Three rounds of treatment later and still I find no relief! I learn that when a doctor doesn't know the cause of a rash, he or she labels it *contact dermatitis.* Not satisfied with simply treating my symptoms, I want to understand *why* this is happening to me! Once I identify the cause or causes, then I can eliminate them!

I look back over the past twenty-five years and wonder if my agoraphobia, hysterectomy, and skin rashes can possibly be related. Perhaps what makes me sick has a common denominator! I start by listing all the things with which my skin comes into contact on a daily basis. I'm surprised to discover that—on an average day—I come into contact with over five hundred different chemicals!

I used hand wash, shower gel, shampoo, deodorant, body lotion, bar soap, toothpaste, hair styling gel, perfume, eyeliner, mascara, makeup, and lipstick—all personal care and household products—and all before breakfast! Then there's the dishwashing detergent, window and household cleaners, disinfect for the bathtub, toilet, and sink, and more...

It's unbelievable how many different chemicals my skin comes in contact with every day!

They say a little knowledge can be a dangerous thing. All this time I assumed that our skin is an impermeable protective barrier that keeps the good stuff in and the bad stuff out. I couldn't have been more wrong, as my research shows that our skin absorbs whatever substances—good or bad—come into contact with it!

Additional research leads me to realize that all of these products contain toxic chemicals that *denature* protein. This means that these toxic chemicals modify the molecular structure—especially via heat, acid, alkali, or ultraviolet radiation—of a protein or DNA, so as to destroy or diminish some of its original properties.

In short, these toxic chemicals change how we look, and not in a good way, by increasing the appearance of age spots, brown spots, wrinkles, sagging skin, and puffy eyes. In addition, they can cause a plethora of ailments—including hormone disruption, joint pain, skin reactions, allergies, depression, headaches, chest pains, ear infections, chronic fatigue, dizziness, loss of sleep, early puberty, hyperactivity, irritability, behavioral changes, violent coughing, vomiting, cancer, heart attacks, blindness, and even death!

What a frightening *aha!* moment when I realize everything my skin comes into contact with that can affect my life so dramatically. It turns out my medical issues have been caused by a combination of chemical toxins built up over an extended period of time. This causes a breakdown in my immune system and hormone disruption.

Suddenly, the fact that I started menstruating at eleven and had a thyroid problem makes sense, as both are hormone-related. All those bubble baths and all that tooth brushing creates hormone disruption! Bubble bath liquids and toothpaste contain substances such as sodium hydroxide—which is the same as lye!, triclosan—a pesticide, and propylene glycol, a.k.a. anti-freeze.

In addition, I discover through my research that, since 1938, the U.S. government does not regulate or control what's used in cosmetics sold in this country. That means products may contain *any* chemical substance and manufacturers are *not* required to list them as ingredients.

The Solution: AlphaZelle To The Rescue

Now that I know I'm chemically sensitive and have severely damaged my skin, my first job is to eliminate toxic ingredients from my life. I begin by going through all my products, and boy do I have a rude awakening! Every single product I use has toxic chemicals in it—with no exceptions!

By this point I've learned that *chemical sensitivity* and/or *toxic overload* eventually damage our alpha, or *mother*, cells—situated at the very base of the skin. These cells are responsible for periodically forming new skin cells which replace the dead cells that slough off on a daily basis.

As damaged alpha cells send increasingly more damaged new cells to the surface of our skin, these unhealthy cells eventually become fine lines and wrinkles, brown or age spots, sagging skin, puffy eye bags, and many other embarrassing skin conditions.

I realize my rashes will *never* clear up unless I repair my deep alpha cells. For me to get healthy and address my problems I need to use products with *no* toxic chemicals in them.

My search for safe, non-toxic products begins, but despite looking in health food stores and natural companies, I find no totally clean products. Even the ones labeled "natural" or "organic" include chemicals and fragrances!

Eventually I realize the only way to guarantee what's in the products I use is to formulate my own!

During my research, I'm fortunate to develop a relationship with a few cosmetic chemists willing to work with me. They help me experiment with powerful and safe active ingredients, and to develop toxin-free preservative systems that will have a long shelf life.

We begin to develop products that perform as advertised, feed the skin with proper nutrition that accelerates healing, and repairs the mother/alpha cells that are toxically overloaded. We start with a few products that can help as many people as possible, including a hand wash, shower gel, shampoo, conditioner, body lotion, facial cleanser, and facial moisturizer.

I name our company AlphaZelle—Alpha for "first" and Zelle for "cell," because this is where real health truly begins. Over the years, we're able to fine-tune our products and use the safest, most powerful active ingredients. Now, after ten years, we have over sixty different "clean" products that don't cause hormone disruption or immune system issues.

Unfortunately, I will probably always be *chemically sensitive*, even though my alpha cells continually heal and constantly send healthy new cells to my skin's surface. However, I can't remember now the last time I had a headache, lacked energy or ambition, or experienced rashes, since my skin has responded so well after many years of feeding it the proper nutrition that our products provide.

I now know how important it is to live a toxin-free life—I only wish I'd learned this earlier!

It's become my mission to educate others so that they and their children don't experience the kind of torment and confusion I did. The most important thing I learned is that I must read ingredient labels. Since our skin absorbs everything it comes into contact with, all ingredients should be as pure as the food we eat.

If I don't think I'd eat it, I won't put it on my skin! I'm profoundly aware that some companies don't want me to know what's in their products and will cleverly disguise toxic ingredients by combining them into a "proprietary blend" with a name I cannot identify, or rename an ingredient to make it sound safe.

Also, companies are not required to disclose the chemical makeup of fragrances, or to list impurities or contaminants. If an ingredient list causes any doubt, I err on the side of caution and keep looking for a cleaner product. I formulate my products with therapeutic food grade essential oils instead of synthetic fragrances.

Now a happy, healthy human being, I love helping toxically overloaded people and their pets return to a more normal life! Also, through AlphaZelle, I help parents prevent their babies and children from becoming chemically sensitive, and assist young people to retain their youthful appearance as they grow older.

I truly love this journey of healthy, vibrant living as we continue to expand our company. Now totally chemical free from A to Z, I know my good health starts with AlphaZelle!

ABOUT THE AUTHOR: Dale's many hats throughout the years include those of bookkeeper, bank teller, stay-at-home mom, networker, artist, caregiver and entrepreneur. While searching for a remedy for her own itchy, painful rashes, Dale joined numerous wellness companies from 1993-2003. Her passion was ignited when she discovered that many of the products she used contained toxic ingredients that caused her chemical sensitivity. This led to her current mission to educate consumers about how to find safer products and replace toxic ones with healthy, eco-friendly versions, and AlphaZelle was born! AlphaZelle offers healthy, eco-friendly, toxin-free (clean and green!) household products for the whole family, including pets.

Dale F. Schock
AlphaZelle LLC
www.alphazelle.com
dale@alphazelle.com
973-288-1971

Remembering Me

Jennifer Britt

I can't stop in time! I watch in horror as my Jeep's red hood wrinkles up as easily as I crumple a newspaper in my hand. The deafening crunch and eardrum-splitting squeal of wrenching, grinding metal is followed by the smell of burnt rubber from my tires as the car swivels 180° forcefully, like a deformed toy.

One of the tires blows with a *pop!* and my radiator exhales steam with a *hiss* as the Jeep's engine drops from its compartment onto the pavement and *wham!*—my head hits the driver's side window and I'm free.

No time...no space...no body...just floating...

Somewhere, faintly, I hear sound, which tugs at my attention and calls for my return. Traveling through a black tunnel that narrows the closer I get, the voice calling my name becomes louder and more insistent until I rejoin my body and realize my boyfriend Kevin's voice has been my bridge back from the oh-so-thin veil dividing life from death.

In dream-like slow motion I watch as an unknown woman—fear and apprehension written all over her face—pries open my car door. Her expression dissolves into relief as she discovers I'm alive.

I hear fire truck and ambulance sirens nearing, though they sound strangely muted and distant, as if my ears are listening from the bottom of a cavernous crevasse deep within my body. It's like I'm peering out from far inside my head although my vision is sharp and crystal clear.

Mental note: my Jeep is pointing in the wrong direction! The windshield of the other car, several feet away, is cracked where the driver's head struck it and he lies slumped over his steering wheel, inert.

Is he dead? wonders my mind, which feels oddly detached from my body.

My hand wanders to feel a large lump forming on my throbbing head. I painstakingly try to make sense of my surroundings and flash back to the last scenes in my memory. I'd picked up Kevin from work and, in high spirits, we were driving to retrieve my five year-old daughter Marina from daycare.

It's October 29, and we have a pre-Halloween date night planned! As we discuss our evening plans, a blur of light flashes in the corner of my eye, and I see far out in the intersection to my left a car barreling toward us. It does not stop for the red light.

He's driving at least sixty mph! My mind reels with disbelief. *Why isn't he slowing down? Why doesn't he see us? Is he drunk?* In surreal slow motion, a split-second before impact, I look down into the other car and realize the driver isn't wearing his seatbelt.

As I return to consciousness, the knowledge that I don't want to leave Marina alone in the world shocks my mind into action. The paramedics arrive and want to strap me onto a gurney and take me to the hospital, but I refuse.

"What time is it?" I ask frantically. "Does anyone have a cell phone I can use to call the daycare? I have to let them know I'm ok and that I'll be late!"

Nothing else matters but getting to Marina. Worried that I'm inconveniencing the daycare staff, or worse—that I will let Marina down because they'll close before I arrive, my mind struggles to find a solution.

Not exactly the fun date night we had planned! After picking up Marina and a trip to the emergency room, we arrive home with pain and anti-inflammatory medications, and an admonition to stay alert for symptoms of concussion.

Dazed And Confused

The following Monday my entire body feels more bruised and battered than it did the night of the accident. In too much pain to work, and overwhelmed by the phone calls I know I have to make to the insurance company, I call my boss and relate details of my accident, feeling guilty that I can't go to work.

A few days later I realize something is very wrong. The pain is worse, and my mind and body don't seem to be communicating with each other. I can't think straight. I lose my balance easily and bump into furniture constantly. I remember events from before the accident, but very little since.

Previously an extremely organized, highly functioning intelligent person, I begin to experience extreme difficulty accomplishing mundane daily chores. I attempt to cook a meal and find myself walking away and forgetting the task at hand. Several times I nearly set the kitchen on fire.

It's difficult to stay within the lanes on the road when driving. I have to write myself reminder notes, directions to and from, the time to pick up Marina after school—all because I can't trust myself to remember such details!

When people speak I see their mouths moving, but my brain can't decipher their words. It's as if they're speaking a foreign language. My hormones become unruly and I'm an emotionally violent roller coaster who ricochets wildly from calmness to unwarranted rage or lengthy crying episodes—in the span of seconds. I lose seventeen pounds in three weeks.

Severe insomnia settles in. Unable to sleep at night, yet barely able to stay awake during the day, my body hurts *everywhere* all the time.

I spend the following eighteen months in the offices of a plethora of allopathic medical practitioners, including a primary physician, physiotherapist, massage therapists, two physical therapists, a speech and cognitive therapist, a psychologist, a neuro-optometrist, a dentist specializing in temporomandibular joint disorder (TMJD), and a neuropsychologist.

I receive a litany of diagnoses and prognoses, including mild traumatic brain injury, speech and cognitive dysfunction, midline brain shift, fibromyalgia, chronic pain syndrome, chronic fatigue syndrome, irritable bowel syndrome, and TMJD, along with accompanying medications and therapies. I spend every week at numerous medical appointments with a single goal in mind: to get back my life and return to normal!

I graduated from massage therapy school just three months prior to my accident, and work as a massage therapist in a very busy clinic. I specialize in providing neuromuscular massage therapy for people injured in car and work-related accidents. The irony of my situation is profound.

Prompted to attend massage school through a series of serendipitous experiences, my entire life had fallen effortlessly into place as I finally found my life's calling. An excellent therapist with a highly developed intuitive sense of touch, I absolutely love my job.

Clients, shocked at how I always find and treat elusive pain patterns, call me the "body whisperer." I quickly developed a reputation for adeptly addressing complex musculoskeletal issues. I love my co-workers, have a terrific boss, and earn a prosperous income. It's of paramount importance to get my life back on track and return to work!

After eighteen months of seemingly endless medical appointments, attended with the belief they'll lead to my eventual recovery, I receive a death blow from my insurance company's physician.

"I'm sorry, but none of your current treatments will be of further benefit to you," he announces bluntly after a cursory physical exam and review of my medical records. "I'm recommending the insurance company stop paying for any further medical treatments, and that you simply accept your current limitations and learn to live with them."

Magical Results

Devastated, I relate my situation to one of my physical therapists the following week. Without hesitation she refers me to Eileen, an intuitive energy healer. Cautiously optimistic after an initial assessment, Eileen shares that she can help me, but wants to treat me in conjunction with another therapist who specializes in other forms of energetic bodywork.

The result is magical! After receiving two highly specialized energetic healing sessions I experience a complete and total recovery from every single diagnosis and symptom!

Rather than feel angry or blame a medical approach that didn't work for me, I'm overjoyed at my renewed health, and excited to learn everything I can about intuition, alternative holistic medicine, and energetic bodywork and healing techniques.

I take classes in clairvoyance, intuition, energy healing, channeling, and other healing modalities, and discover along the way much more than anticipated. Slowly I begin to remember other traumatic injuries, near-death experiences, and early childhood interactions with angels, archangels, spirit guides, and other non-physical beings that somehow I'd forgotten.

The skills, tools, and techniques I learn, and the certifications I earn enable me to heal long-forgotten wounds and reconnect to my soul. Soon I realize I'm not learning anything new at all, because with each new technique, skill, or modality, I'm aware that I'm actually *remembering* what seems more like ancient knowledge.

This becomes a shocking revelation—it's as if I'm piecing back together parts of myself that have been within my consciousness forever, but that I lost or forgot over time through various injuries and traumas experienced during my life.

My early life situation taught me I wasn't safe in the world. I couldn't trust others, myself, and certainly not God. Feeling lost, so very alone and unsafe, I made both a conscious and unconscious decision somewhere around the age of three to hide my light, exuberance, joy, and gifts—in essence, I became invisible.

Invisibility served to keep my consciousness intact as a child, but as my search for healing and wholeness resurrects memories of numerous traumatic injuries and near-death experiences, I see how that invisibility limited me from expressing myself fully and authentically in the world. I was so literally *invisible* that the other guy's car barreled into my Jeep at sixty miles per hour!

I begin to comprehend that while I can easily choose to attach myself to "woe is me" stories and use them as a crutch to stay stuck in my past for the rest of my life, I can also choose to perceive them as gifts delivered with great purpose. Although I intended initially to learn healing techniques and intuitive skills for myself only, it occurs to me now that perhaps I experienced this accident in order to learn these tools to help others.

Turns out they become the perfect tools for me to express my own life purpose! Finally, I embrace the true magnitude of who I am and why I'm here: I'm a *life architect!* I begin to offer *SoulPrint,* a successful transformational process that helps clients explore life as a whole through the lens of their larger soul perspective. Through my program, they heal traumatic experiences, reclaim their power, illuminate their soul's path and purpose, and restructure their life to align with this true purpose.

I know now that whatever issues we struggle with internally always manifest themselves in our external lives in such a way that our soul is able to utilize the lesson to grow and evolve. Life unfolds exactly as it is meant to and there are no accidents—only the perfection of our souls' expression of a higher purpose, something to which I reawakened when *remembering me...*

ABOUT THE AUTHOR: Jennifer Britt, a "life architect," draws on 20+ years' experience as an intuitive spiritual counselor, energy healer, and certified professional coach to masterfully guide her clients through a highly specialized transformational process. She helps them discover their soul's most authentic expression, clear the blocks to their success, and restructure their lives. Jennifer knows that when her clients are challenged they grow beyond what they think is possible - and when they commit fully to the process, they see powerful, measurable results quickly. Work with Jennifer and invest in *yourself and the rest of your life!*

Rev. Jennifer Britt, B.A., C.P.C.
Jennifer Britt Coaching
www.jenniferbrittcoaching.com
jenniferbritt.coaching@gmail.com
719-432-7240

Where The Magic Happens

Diane Metivier

"I give you permission to take care of *you!*" is all she says, and I'm *all* ears!

Why does it take another woman—a stranger really—to tell me this for me to listen? I wonder. Uttered by motivational speaker Lisa Nichols during a three-day event in Atlantic City, N.J., in March 2012, this one sentence is literally how I begin to allow myself to care for *me*.

"You must fill your cup so you can pour into others—it's not a selfish, but a *selfless*, thing you are doing!" Nichols continues. "By serving yourself, you can better serve others."

A first time mom at forty-four, I love the work I do, but feel lost—as both a wife and a mother. Guilty about taking this time to nurture myself and to build my practice, this is the first time I'm away from my four year-old son Matthew overnight and I realize how much I've forgotten what makes me *me*.

That person who knows she needs to nurture herself seems to have disappeared. In a bad place personally, I don't feel fulfilled in the way I *know* is possible. Frequently a dear friend reminds me to get out of my head and into my heart. However, when I want to do things for myself, I simply can't give myself permission to be that selfish.

Afraid to say it out loud, I feel very alone. I crave the kind of social, emotional, and spiritual stimulation one doesn't get at home, but rather comes from the company of like-minded women with whom I can work, network, and be friends. In short, I miss my girlfriend time!

Meanwhile, raising Matthew is a life-altering experience—never did I imagine my heart could be so full of love and gratitude—and I don't want to miss a thing! Much of my guilt is clearly self-inflicted.

However, at this age I no longer possess the vitality formerly associated with my upbeat and silly personality. Despite the joy that Matthew brings to my life, I feel unbalanced–as if I'm serving everyone except myself. I need desperately to find a way to do things differently and more efficiently at work, so I can spend as much time as possible with Matthew and my husband Frank.

The People Pleaser

My parents, strict but fair, are loving, supportive, and caring. Dad is retired Air Force and there are rules. I'm taught not to disrespect my parents or elders, and to do what I'm told and follow rules without question.

Going against the rules has consequences. Challenging the opinion or direction of my parents is not an option–not that I ever thought about doing so. It's not repressive, but neither is it a democracy, and I don't question that. One of five kids, I conform happily to win my parents approval and respect.

Always I work hard and do my best–I want to make them proud of me! I never get into trouble and want people to like me. I believe fighting is bad. Arguing is bad. Disagreements or conflict are bad. I avoid conflict like the plague.

I recall my parents occasionally raising their voices behind their bedroom door–my room is across from theirs–after my siblings and I are in bed. Terrified that they're angry at each other, I fear they don't love each other anymore. Insecure and unsafe when this happens, I realize they're everything to me–my security, stability, my whole world!

Even though these arguments dissipate quickly and everything is always fine, moments of conflict in my life open a floodgate of emotions that bring me back to those incidents. I develop low self esteem–but don't know why, since I cannot recall being made to feel like I'm not enough. Still, that is how I feel.

Old School

Serious depression hits when I'm in my thirties and lasts a number of years, during which it's difficult dealing with life. Often, if I'm not included or accepted in something, it devastates to me to the point where I come totally undone.

I begin to see lots of examples of my lack of self-acceptance and self-love. A terrific athlete with a four point average throughout school and college, I'm fit and healthy. I win awards. In short, I'm the whole package–but inside I believe I'll never measure up or be good enough—no matter what.

My parents always tell me "we want you to do your best, we always support you," and I know they are sincere. One day, my mother shares with me the following story:

A very bright child, I'm known to "correct" a teacher or two. Some teachers are more accepting of this than others, though by mother's account I'm dead on correct in each instance.

Evidently, one teacher in sixth grade becomes very threatened by me and goes out of her way to be as nasty and critical of me as possible. On a mission to show me that I don't know more than she does and to teach me a lesson, she puts me down, and publicly humiliates and embarrasses me without mercy until she leaves due to disability.

My mother recalls how other teachers approach her to apologize for this teacher's inappropriate and mean behavior, and swears that from that time on I begin to question myself. I second guess myself, ask for a lot of reassurance on my work and other decisions, and am not confident acting on my own.

Shocked, it dawns on me now how this teacher broke me and my spirit, and I didn't even realize it!

The Real *Me*

"You are enough!" Lisa Nichols continues in her motivational speech.

Wow, I never really understood that until this moment, I muse. Always I look for external validation and recognition, and compare myself to others to measure where I am in my journey.

I'm looking in the wrong direction! I realize suddenly. *It's more important that I move inward and follow my heart, trust my gut, and keep living the life I've always lived—by being honest, loyal, good, and loving! It doesn't matter if others disagree with me or my decisions—it's ok, my opinion is good enough!*

This *aha!* moment changes me forever. I know I have to change how I think about things, and listen—*really listen*—to what my intuition and gut are saying, and to trust it! When I look back at the times when my gut told me to do something but I dismissed it—only to find out afterward that my intuition was dead on—I realize I *must* change my way of thinking.

During this period of self-discovery I reassess my work life. My firm—where I've been for the past fourteen years since I started my business—is going through a transition process and it becomes very clear that the time has come for me to move on.

I sense that something has to change, but don't know how it will play out. The thought of going it alone terrifies me—I'm used to partnership, collaboration, and the safety net these provide. For the first time I realize the financial cost to my family if I continue to play it safe.

Although I've given my word that I'll go a certain way, when all is revealed, it's clear not only that this is impractical, but also that it doesn't make good financial sense. Plus, I know I won't be happy. Soon I realize I'm simply scared of the unknown. Fearful of letting the relationship go because it's safe, I understand I have to cut the cord of dependency even though I enjoy the team approach and feeling like I belong.

My gut screams it's time to go, but at first I can't take a call from the owner of the firm, with whom I have an important work relationship. I don't know if I'm strong enough to stand up to him— I've never before questioned or challenged him—and feel compelled not to disappoint him.

Shortly after, however, for the first time, I stand up for myself and speak my truth to someone I consider both my mentor and a friend. I respect this man, and the old Diane wouldn't have wanted to rock the boat, fearful that others would be upset with me, or think badly of me. A new experience for us both, it's not a very comfortable one, but the result is that I begin to search for new alternatives...

Can I do this on my own? I worry. *I've never been without support! Can I run my own office and do all the things I normally delegate?*

One Step At A Time

Time passes and events occur that simply put one stone right in front of me along the path, over and over. All I have to do is take that first step and then the next. I couldn't have planned it any better if I'd tried! When all is said and done, I leave my office with the only firm I've ever known to move into my home office the week Matthew starts Pre-K.

Grateful to work from home, I take Matthew to and from school each day—an immeasurable blessing! The first of many, I find out later. Finally, I recognize how I'd been selling myself short!

I can do whatever I need to and it will all work out! I have only to step into my full power and know and trust that I honor and believe in myself! I learn along the way that I can break away from the herd if I put my full faith and trust in myself first and don't allow the opinions or disappointment of others to sway my decision.

As difficult or uncomfortable as it is, I learn also to trust my intuition no matter how painful and scary this seems. Now I put myself and my family first, and not someone else, which is the pattern I exhibited up until recently. I know what's right for me, and commit myself to staying true to that. I no longer allow old habits or fears to get in the way!

Now I assume a position of empowerment in every area of my life. No longer do I believe that everyone else has the answers, or knows better. This stretches me in ways I've never even considered! Such an incredibly empowering experience provides me with a new mantra: "Get comfortable with being uncomfortable!" *That's* where the magic happens!

ABOUT THE AUTHOR: As a professional, Diane's "hands on" approach spans 15 years experience assisting individuals with getting back to basics with their budgeting—including finding hidden dollars in their current budget—and removing *fear* from their finances. Diane's *goal is to* steer individuals toward getting where they want to go financially in order to realize their dreams. Diane, also the author of five children's books, seeks to inspire and empower women and children through education. Her goal—through workshops for children of varied ages—includes promoting a healthy relationship with money.

Diane Metivier
"Inspiring Women and Children Financially"
diane@inspiringwomenfinancially.com
www.inspiringwomenfinancially.com
609-526-5864

Mission Accomplished
Yolanda Russo

I notice the young college-age girl immediately and see the dark circles under her eyes as she walks into the spa one Saturday morning while I'm standing at the front desk helping people check in.

"I have this headache that won't go away, and want to see if I can get a massage," she says.

Immediately I call for front desk backup and take her in. Turns out Melissa's migraines started long ago and she's visited many doctors—including a neurosurgeon—but no one can help her. Rather, they all agree to drug her and hope her headaches will disappear.

She sees auras and can't concentrate during her classes. When back in her dorm, she sleeps. She's a good student, though I don't know how she does it. I work with Melissa for several months, then request that she ask her doctor to lower the dosage of her migraine medication.

A few months later I ask her to do the same again, and finally she's pain and drug free. I work with her physically, but also coach her on how to handle the onset of a migraine to minimize its duration. I advise her that her migraine episodes will return occasionally, and that she'll need to deal with that.

Forced Resignation

Growing up in eastern European Poland during the communist regime, I suffer from migraines for two years before the pain becomes so severe that I'm bedridden at age eighteen. That entire summer I can't hold anything in my stomach and my headache is so painful I cannot bear to hear even a pin fall.

In 1980's Poland we all face challenges—mainly with the way we are forced to think and live. We can watch and read only censored information, and I grow up with only three television channels–one government-run, a movie channel (with mostly old movies), and a leisure channel with stories for kids. Mickey Mouse airs every night at 7:30 p.m., and I don't want to miss it, because if I do I won't see it again.

Most people here are ok with this–they believe it's the life they must live. I'm different–I don't like any of it and don't believe someone else should control our future, but cannot say anything to anyone because no one can do anything about it. As I grow older, the stress builds, resulting in severe migraines by my teenage years.

During this period in Poland, migraine is considered an attitude problem, not a disease. Doctors test me, but can't find any medical problem. Diagnosed as a healthy individual, the current popular belief is that people choose to have migraines to avoid their social life or to pretend to be sick so others feel sorry for them.

On my own with my migraines, the medical doctors having determined I'm a healthy adult, my family and friends declare I'm making this up and distance themselves from me. Everybody leaves me alone, including my mother, and nobody comes around. This is how people in Europe think–the doctor is God, and medicine is all there is.

At this point, sick as a dog, I want to die from the pain. Fortunately I have good moments, and during these glimpses of light I arrive at the conclusion that mainstream medicine has its limitations, and that since even doctors are turning their backs on me I will have to take care of it myself.

No one is going to help me, I think, *not a doctor–not anyone from my family–if I don't help myself.* Cleared of any disease–and if I'm not sick, then I'm not going to be cured–I decide to take matters into my own hands and choose to control my stress to see if my migraines get any better.

Stress and tension start the vicious cycle of pain, so I learn about yoga, meditation, herbs, massage, and even magnetic therapy. While in college I take pre-med courses to apply later to medical school. I want to become a holistic doctor and help people like me who are literally rejected by everyone and perceived as lazy or making up their disease.

While studying biology and chemistry it becomes clear to me that our brains are capable of being sick when our body chemistry is out of alignment. When optimal conditions are met–including enough oxygen in the blood to push healthy nutrients to areas of the body that need help–the body can cure itself. I learn also that our bodies are perfect and want to stay in constant balance (homeostasis). When out of balance, our body forces us to lie down and/or become sick to protect itself from further damage.

Things suddenly start making sense, and the more I control my stress, the longer between episodes of debilitating pain. I focus more on the positive to avoid stress and negative thoughts, and train my brain to converse with *me* when my tension builds:

You'll pay for this tomorrow with a migraine, I think, and usually prove to be right. Meditation and breathing exercises become a starting point for managing my migraines without medication. Proud of myself for my success, I decide I need to help others deal with this "life destroying" disorder. After finishing college, I set out to leave my country for the U.S. to look for an opportunity for a better life.

The Natural Face Lift

I'm young enough at twenty-seven to make decisions without realizing how very hard and brave is my undertaking, and in 1990 I make the dramatic move. I don't expect anything to go wrong because, well, you don't know what you don't know. Although I speak no English when I arrive, I complete an ESL course after six months. This proves to be the starting point of my journey into the future!

As my English improves, I take refresher courses in biology, anatomy, and physiology. I can't afford medical school so I apply to a physician assistant program but do not get accepted. Alone in this country, I don't have much choice but to work and go to school simultaneously.

I attend school for seven years and work in the medical field as a medical laboratory technician, testing blood for doctors so they can diagnose people. It's clear they have to prove it through the blood sample or via a scan in order to diagnose. Then they medicate, and off you go. It's here I begin to question why if they don't see it, they can't diagnose it.

I decide to attend a year-long massage therapy school program, and work during the day while I attend classes at night. I graduate in 1996 and am on my way to do what I decided to do—help those whom conventional medicine has failed. The next several years I work with people suffering from migraines and fibromyalgia, among other conditions.

Very happy with what's happening, I'm using all kinds of unconventional modalities—from Reiki to magnetic therapy to visualization techniques—and people experience amazing results. I'm on the path to helping people!

Next my journey takes another evolutionary turn. I set out to build a center for beauty and healing that opens its doors in 2001, right before 9/11. People—stressed and very scared following 9/11— are not sure what's next. I ask God to help by sending me clients who really need my assistance. I open my door and that's exactly what happens.

As I start working in my newly expanded spa business, I discover that women's faces look wrinkle-free when I'm done working on their necks to relieve pain—my routine treatment for headaches.

I realize I need to explore a skin care program to become licensed and able to work on clients' faces. I decide *Natural Face Lift* is an appropriate name for this new and exciting treatment—not only does it make clients' faces look younger and smoother, it reduces stress in their whole body and thus helps relieve their neck tension. Another step down the path of helping people feel and look better!

Many clients come to me complaining of unhappiness in a relationship or at work. Unfortunately they aren't doing anything to change their situations, but I find that after improving their appearance they instantly feel good and agree to make changes in their lives. Once they realize it's up to them to make their life better and happier, it's easier for them to maintain a positive attitude.

Natural Face Lift becomes my staple to success, and sixteen years later I focus only on facial treatments. Every day I see its amazing results: a peaceful face and relaxed body. Women look ten years younger simply by releasing the tension from their forehead and jaw line, which erases their wrinkles.

My extensive knowledge of biology, chemistry, and anatomy allow me to coach my clients about nutrition, stretching, and relaxation while giving them a facial. This value-added service empowers women because I teach them what to do and hand them the tools with which to do it. Many discover home remedies and self-help methods that deal with skin care. Now they know they can fix most of the things that make them unhappy—such as forehead lines, marionette lines, and crow's feet—and re-glow their skin on their own.

Epilogue

Two years later Melissa comes to visit me to thank me for giving her life back. She's working now and very successful. It was an accident—or so it seemed—that she came to shop in the mall that day and ended up finding a new lease on life.

The irony is that I wasn't supposed to be working that day when Melissa made the decision to open the door and help herself. She figured she'd take a chance, walked in, and a chain reaction took place. There is a force that drives us to our destiny, and those who make a choice to stop dwelling on the negatives will succeed in whatever life may have in store for them.

I am a prime example of that, because I make conscious choices and stick to them. I know we can *choose* to complain about something and never be happy, we can *choose* to blame everyone else and never heal, or we can *choose* to do something about our lives and live happily ever after. I always remind clients to believe in themselves and not to depend on anyone to help them but themselves.

My next step in life will be to offer a licensed training program to teach professionals my proprietary system so they can go out and help more people than I can reach on my own. I won't be stopped by anything or anyone or settle for less until it's mission accomplished! I'm on the path to success, and success isn't measured in dollars—it's measured in smiles!

ABOUT THE AUTHOR: Yolanda Russo is the founder and creator of Beauty On Command: Natural Facelift Made Easy. With almost 20 years of experience in the beauty and wellness industry and a degree in Biology, Yolanda applies her extensive knowledge and experience in the use of state of the art European tools and technology in delivering the finest skin care treatments. No surgery. No fillers. All botanical and safe ingredients applied in a scientifically choreographed way. Yolanda is a genius when it comes to preserving one's beauty, youthful looks and radiance utilizing simple, sensible, and easy to follow natural modalities.

Yolanda Russo
www.speranzi.co
www.beautyoncommand.com
yolanda@speranzifacial.com
973-228-7727

Why Me?
Linda Newton

Home alone, I grab my five-and-a-half month old pregnant belly as pain shoots through me and blood begins to stain my pants. Shock and disbelief hold me captive for a moment—it's clear something is terribly wrong!—as my head spins.

What's going on? I've finally started to feel human again! *What to do?* I just left my day shift nursing job to come home and fix dinner. Healthy and active, I really want this baby, as does my husband Hank.

I call him first—as if guided by some divine source—but he's unavailable! I leave a message. It doesn't occur to me to call 911. I grab extra padding and my purse and, in a daze, drive myself back to the hospital where I work in labor and delivery.

I'm not bleeding profusely, but the pain intensifies and I'm so afraid the placenta is separating from the wall of the uterus (placenta abruptia). Unfortunately, I know a little bit too much about these things. Also, I know I have to get to the hospital so they can to do something to save this baby!

Even though I'm an obstetrics nurse, this pregnancy thing is a new experience. I arrive at the hospital, a million questions lodged in my brain.

What if I lose this baby? Where's Hank? Why am I here alone? It seems that whenever there's a crisis, I'm alone! Why me, God, why me? What did I do to deserve this? What's wrong with me?

Our baby girl is born and dies on March 9. My heart a black hole, my eyes swollen from crying, grieving this loss proves difficult for us both and, of course, for our families. It's our first baby, about whom everyone was so excited.

Several months later, pregnant again, everyone has high hopes. After all, there's no reason why placenta abruptia will happen again. However, I am more cautiously excited this time.

Just when I'm starting to feel better at five-and-a-half months, my contractions begin. I deliver a fourteen ounce baby girl, who dies thirteen minutes after birth on December 13.

Two losses, same year. Stunned that this could happen twice, I'm headed for a dark night of the soul as I begin to question myself. Self doubt, depression, and a poor self image take over. *Why me?* I moan silently. *Why am I a powerless victim of the fates? Here I'm an obstetrics nurse and I see women giving birth every day—it's part of my job! I see women come through who care less about having a baby and those who take pregnancy for granted. Some are annoyed that they're pregnant, some sleep as their babies emerge, and a few try unsuccessfully to abort their pregnancy.*

Before, I wanted to assist them, make their pregnancies as painless as possible, teach them Lamaze, help them through labor, and take care of them afterward. Now I'm devastated and ask again *why me?*

I feel terrible for Hank. He grows more silent, moving inward. Guilt and shame hit me hard. *Why did he choose this loser?* I shut down, avoid communication, and continue to go through life robotically. Never overtly suicidal, nevertheless I have times when I simply don't want to wake up.

Empowered Me

"Stay out of it Alice," my father says. "Linda must learn to stand up for herself!"

We live in an apartment complex and every morning I walk to the bus stop skipping, humming, and carrying my lunch box. Five years old and on my way to kindergarten, one day I'm ambushed by this four year-old boy who lives in my complex. He jumps out of the bushes, pushes me down, grabs my lunch box, runs around the corner and drops it, scattering food everywhere.

Scared, I cry, pick up my lunch, and get on the bus.

I tell my parents about this bullying, of course. My mother is beside herself with wanting to help me, but my good German father insists I must learn to deal with this on my own. I come to learn later that his mother died when he was only five, and that he was on his own from a very early age, especially since his father worked all the time.

This routine happens every day. I hate going to the bus stop and wonder *why isn't anyone helping me?* The anxiety—I have a knot in my stomach and palpitations—is overwhelming, until one day I've finally had it and I haul off and smack him with my lunch box!

He cries to his mother about what a bully I am! Elated that I took back my power *and* my lunch, I'm happy that day and so proud that I finally stood up for myself. Boy, is my dad happy, too. The bully never bothers me again.

My teen years are filled with fun and self-loathing. Self conscious because I have bad acne on my face, I hate looking in the mirror. *Who's going to befriend someone that looks like me?* I wonder.

One day my mother and I are in a store and she meets a friend who's holding a young child. The little boy studies me for a few moments, then looks at his mom.

"Does she have chicken pox?" he asks her.

I run out of the store crying, hating my looks—hating everyone!

However, I do learn about inner peace during these years. As awful as I feel I look, I love school and people. Also, I love to laugh and to be just a little bit quirky. Cheerleading proves to be my outlet. It's exciting to cheer with my friends and for my friends on the team!

I join clubs, and go to parties and sleepovers with special girlfriends. In my junior and senior years I'm captain of the cheerleading squad, secretary of the student body, and voted Snowflake Queen. One day, I realize how often I'm in front of people.

Wait a minute, these people are crazy—don't they see my face?

Senior year I'm voted "Best All Around." What an honor! This is the healing turning point for me: *Wow, you can really look past the exterior of someone to what they bring to the table—not physically, but that inner spark!*

I love these years, and how I'm accepted not for how I look but for who I am. I look back now at all I accomplished and see the lessons learned: that there is good in humanity, and how others taught me not to judge a book by its cover.

If At First You Don't Succeed...

Concerned doctors conclude that I have an incompetent cervix—a condition where my cervix can only hold a certain amount of weight before it just opens up—most likely due to my mother taking the hormone DES when pregnant with me.

Hank and I talk about trying again. We both want a baby, but I'm so afraid that if I lose another one, I'll lose my mind! The doctors assure me that if they stitch my cervix the baby will remain inside.

"Linda, you've got to get in bed," my doctor advises when, at six months, the baby starts pulling on the stitches. I retire to bed for four months while my mother takes care of me, and give birth at thirty-seven-and-a-half-weeks to six-pound three-ounce baby Scott! What a joy!

However, Scott encounters breathing difficulties and yellow jaundice.

What are you doing to me? I look up at the sky and lament. *I have this baby and now there's a chance he may not make it?* Suddenly I realize I can do no more. *I stayed in bed to hold onto him,* I think, *but now I have to surrender.* This becomes the moment I let go.

Although Scott isn't an easy baby, he begins to thrive. Four years later, we discover I'm pregnant again. Surprised and delighted, I give birth to healthy eight-pound six-ounce Kristin!

I Never Promised You A Rose Garden

In the fourteen years that follow, my marriage fades, then ends. Lack of communication makes us like passing ships. Divorce is difficult, and becomes a time when I *really* want answers. I read, pray, and find myself asking yet again: *why me?*

The children, now ten and six respectively, are my saving grace. Yet I have much alone time, too, and engage in major soul searching. I begin to realize I've been afraid of living life on my own.

Always I had Mom and Dad who oversaw everything. When I married Hank, my high school boyfriend, it was like the Cinderella complex—I went from Dad to the next man who'd take care of me. *Who's going to do that for me now?*

Worried that I'll stick out like a sore thumb and people will say "oh, that's the divorcee, you can tell by looking at her house," I resolve to cut grass, trim bushes, and make it all work. By not giving in to despair and instead rallying to the situation at hand, I gain a fighting spirit and the confidence that I can make this work. *I can do this,* I vow.

Eventually I realize that the question comes down not to *why me?* but rather *why not me?* I've been looking to be rescued, and begin to understand I must take back my power because no one is going to save me! Rather, it's about choice and responsibility to myself.

It dawns on me that I had a choice to let that kid keep pushing me and taking my lunch or to stand up to him. I had a choice to let the acne keep me from enjoying those super teen years, or to join in, discover what I wanted, and go for it, in spite of how I looked.

I had the choice to move past my self-loathing and feeling not good enough, my initial failure in childbearing, and my failed marriage, and to keep moving forward in a hopeful, positive way.

A big follower of Donna Eden, a pioneer in the field of holistic healing and energy medicine, I become a Reiki master. Always interested in how people think, the choices they make, why they make them, and what their past has to do with their present, I know it's about energy and helping people get in touch with their own energies.

A natural cheerleader for my clients, I'm not the magic fairy who's going to wave the magic wand. Instead, I give my clients tools to help them access their internal strengths, and they let me know which ones work best to make their lives better.

Now happily married for more than twenty years, and with two beautiful children and five grandchildren, I ask myself *what can I learn from this?* instead of *why me?*

ABOUT THE AUTHOR: A registered nurse and licensed mental health counselor, Linda partners with clients to help them increase their health and well-being. Through her private counseling practice Linda guides clients to become aware of what works and what doesn't in their lives, and assists them to design a course of action that resonates with their own truth. Linda loves exploring new territories for herself such as qigong, zentangle art, yoga, and writing. "Life is about learning," Linda notes. "May I never lose my curiosity, as forward thinking and growth is what I try to bring to my practice and to everyone I meet."

Linda Newton, LPC, RNC
newtonlnd@aol.com
908-334-3662 in Central NJ

Divine Acceptance
Of Sensual Wisdom
Denise Elizabeth Byron

"Please stay on the phone with me!" I beg my friend. Night is falling as I navigate the interstate through the downpour.

I know my voice sounds far away and flat—my life is falling apart! Waves of emotion crash over me as I review the life I've just left behind. Separated from my husband for two months after a year of couples counseling, I wonder: *how can I trust any of my decisions if they've guided me to a dangerous highway covered with water, alone, and moving toward a temporary destination with no plan for the future?*

Told in meditation I should leave before the first snowfall, I know it's time to take these first steps out of the small town where we live. I want to begin a new life in an area where there are more possibilities for the fullest expression of myself and my work.

Nothing prepares me for this agonizing journey and, after saying goodbye to my husband and cats, I sob my way over the mountain roads as a storm brews. The storm hits after I'm out of the mountains, and the rain and snow follow. The gut-wrenching grief of leaving behind all I love distracts me and I don't trust myself not to run the car off the road. *Will this excruciating turmoil swirling inside me ever end?*

An intuitive, passionate, and sensual woman, it's taken me nearly fifty years to be able to reclaim the *me* I was born to be. I hate to admit that I've operated under the umbrella of shame for so long that sometimes I don't see how much I oppress myself with my own thoughts and judgments. Now, by my forty-seventh year, I can no longer allow myself to repress my innate desire for a full and pleasurable life.

In the process, I leave behind twenty-seven years of a good life—

one built with a wonderful man. I loved him, and love him still, as the man with whom I was able to find refuge from an abusive childhood. I had a wonderful, comfortable life—a nice home, part-time work, great friends, fun dinner parties. We supported each other with grace through multiple family dramas, life changes, illness, and more.

However, our journey together needs to change as the me I buried at age nineteen begins to blossom into the woman I was born to be.

This is not a choice I ever planned on making. I've yet to discover that my journey includes vanquishing the raging inner demons of guilt, shame, and regret during nights shrouded in the kind of dark stillness that happens when you live alone for the first time in your life.

Finding My Way Home

Directed by Archangel Michael—one of my spiritual guides—to a tiny magical home that calls to me, the universe extends much grace at this time of seemingly unending grief.

As someone who experienced childhood parental neglect and physical abuse—and who as a teen was molested and forced into sex by a family member—I had a lot of healing to do. So many layers of guilt and shame cover me that I can't find my way back to myself for a long time.

My marriage is not one of passion; it's one of support. Affectionate with—and there for—each other, we don't explore the full richness of intimate relationship. It's as if we circle the airport waiting for permission to land—for several decades.

I spend years in therapy, take personal growth and development classes, learn about alternative healing modalities, pray, create art, travel on retreats, and work hard to heal. I am nothing if not determined to be one with my full self.

Several weeks after my move, living alone for the first time *ever* in my life, I view myself in the mirror. The truth is, as I look at the fat around my middle and my very full breasts lying against my body—in direct opposition to perky—I feel shame. I regret letting go of the once-toned body I had in high school, and wonder if there will ever be a man who'll find me attractive and want to make love with the passionate woman inside this body.

Then I remember a conversation with a mentor ten years earlier.

"When you're able to look at your naked body in front of a mirror, and love every inch of it, then you'll be able to fulfill your destiny," he advised me.

At the time I could not even grasp what he meant. I've possessed what our culture would call a "middle-aged" body since my twenties. Beset by media-fueled negative programming that literally boggles my mind, I haven't felt good about my physical self since I wore "chubby" sizes from Sears at the age of eight.

Shocked as I look at myself in the mirror again, now I get it! Curvaceous and well-rounded, I carry more weight than is probably healthy for me. But I'm strong and committed to becoming more fit as I age. And, I'm sexy because I feel sexy!

Being prepared and taking the journey are two different things. As it turns out, I have within me and around me the tools to take those faltering first steps. This time of my life is indeed a pilgrimage of remembering, of putting all the pieces of myself back together like some sort of profound scavenger hunt in the wild unknown territories of my heart and soul and body.

Hidden Gems

I want to understand and experience intimacy. In 2001, I begin to learn how to engage the wisdom of the spirit with our sensual nature. It begins with me loving me.

This happens through a sacred sensual embodiment practice, which cultivates and allows sensual/sexual energy to flow. Tapping into my own sexual energy is a most profound experience even though it takes time to heal from the abuse, neglect, rape, etc., and to bring me to the point where most people start.

Shut down from my sexual center up, I feel energy moving through my body right away and it scares me, though my teacher reassures me it's normal. Still, I'm terrified.

My past begins to resurface with a vengeance, and I seek the support of a therapist who understands my commitment to remember my wholeness and to heal. Between my sessions with her and the experience of the moving meditations every week, I begin to awaken the light, love, and soft sensual energy of my body, heart, and soul...of *me!*

This powerful commitment continues to help me reclaim myself each and every time I practice. I access a source filled with the pleasure and joy of remembering myself. I learn that I want to maintain an open heart, but if I'm not connected to my sexual center I won't experience that heart connection.

Every day I discover some hidden gem within myself, something I had forgotten. Each week, an awareness that brings me more confidence and strength surfaces and integrates into my psyche like those outside puzzle pieces that define the bigger picture.

Tears of gratitude fill my eyes as I think of the many lonely nights spent learning about my own energy, wants, and desires. To relax within the embrace of a source far greater than I, and to know I have within me that source, is a profound gift. To understand without a doubt that our true nature is one of pleasure is extraordinary and—truthfully—frightening.

I learn to love my entire self with radical acceptance, make new friends, build my own successful and profitable business, and continue healing a past filled with uncertainty, doubt, and low self-esteem.

Digging out from the pit of shame takes time. When I view the bigger picture that continues to emerge with its colorful puzzle pieces, I see an extraordinary process of unfolding fueled by my innate connection to the divine within.

Delicious Sensual Wisdom

I encourage my own beginner's mind and heart as I allow what is most healing and pleasurable for me to be revealed. I listen and learn from those who have walked this path ahead of me. I read books delivered by wide-eyed UPS drivers who have accidentally broken open the packages. I find the courage to take classes at a sophisticated adult toy store.

I watch videos of loving couples having sex and pleasuring themselves and each other. I talk with friends. I learn things that would have curled my hair if that process had not already started as a result of peri-menopause.

Sensual and alive with vital life force, I experience bliss. At times I invite all of my emotions—including anger and frustration—then consciously let go, allowing my body's wisdom to bring whatever healing is needed in that moment. Honored to connect with my body and the sacred within and around me, I sum it up with one word: *delicious!*

Through what is now called Sensuous Wisdom™, I revel in the energy that moves through me. It's like warm honey pouring throughout my body and nourishing me on every level. My body's undulations open the tight places, my breath deepens, and I relax. My jaw loosens and my shoulders drop. My hips open, and my pelvic floor relaxes, creating an even more pleasurable feeling inside.

But what of my heart? What of the tender places previously encased in shadow and shame? Would they be ready to accept another relationship? Could I begin that exploration? What shall I do now with a life that's just beginning—with so much energy and love to share within this rounded body?

Finding the right partner is daunting. Filling out the form on the internet dating site is surprisingly helpful. I need to know who I am and the type of match I want, even though I don't post it for nearly a year.

Finally, I start seeing a man with whom conversation flows from our first date. He promises there will be plenty of diverse discussion, presence, purpose, pleasure, and passion. My mind, heart, and soul connect in powerful ways and my body overflows with delight.

We continue our exploration of mind, heart, and body. We honor the gift we are to each other. I'm blown wide open as we experience falling in love a little more each day, one day at a time. My heart unlocks and I cry, feeling like I've opened to my core with love, passion, and a gentle healing force that wants me to live—really live! Every cell in my body vibrates with heat, joy, and pure exquisite pleasure.

Prioritizing my personal journey is key as I rebuild my life from the inside out. The waves of emotion still pound at times, but I accept them as I do the ocean tides. I am one with my heart, soul, and body's deep, powerful, divine acceptance of feminine essence and sensual wisdom. And I love her!

ABOUT THE AUTHOR: At age 8, Denise's love of dance was crushed by a teacher who said she was too 'big' to be a performer. Now in her 50's, Denise revels in her curvaceous body as she teaches a powerful movement practice for women who want to feel more sexy, sensual, and confident. The creator of Sensuous Wisdom™ and WISE Women™ Programs, Denise invites women to embrace their beauty and power. With her warm and compassionate presence, she encourages women to let go of past hurts and celebrate their full aliveness. As a Visionary Strategist, she offers unique guidance to help creative entrepreneurs achieve greater fulfillment and success.

Denise Elizabeth Byron
Sensuous Wisdom™ Mentor and Visionary Guide
www.deniseelizabethbyron.com
sensuouswisdom@gmail.com
541-601-9096

Transformational Magic: Creating Common Ground

Kathy Sipple

"In my youthfulness I expressed a foolish surprise that he who had written 'The Origin of Species' should deal with a subject so insignificant as worms...in Nature no agency can be regarded as insignificant, that the most stupendous effects have been produced by the ceaselessly repeated action of small forces." ~ Edward B. Aveling, 'The Religious Views of Charles Darwin'

I kneel in front of my Worm Factory 360 compost bin and place my offerings of a banana peel and eggshells in the top tray. Once again I'm awestruck at the sight and scent of its contents.

I peek inside the lower tray and marvel at finely crumbled bits of newly created moist earth–the color of espresso beans–as the rich, pleasant, earthy scent of compost wafts upward.

Thousands of red wiggler worms (Eisenia fetida) perform transformational magic at my house in Valparaiso, Indiana–Valparaiso means "vale of paradise" in Spanish–every single day! I work at building a garden paradise starting with the best soil possible. My worms, along with a team of supporting microbes, perform biological alchemy and transform my garbage into *love* in the form of organic black gold.

A spiritual seeker, I've searched for–and found–spiritual answers from diverse sources, beginning with my traditional Catholic upbringing and later, a Unity church. I have learned much from Kabbalah, Reiki, yoga, meditation, journaling, tarot, HeartMath, shamanic journeying, Access Bars, *A Course in Miracles* and many more books and lectures on metaphysics.

But what keeps me grounded–literally–is this most basic of activities: vermicomposting, or creating soil with the help of worms. I remember my first encounter with the idea of vermicomposting at my local Earth Day celebration in 2008.

"This soil is alive," a man tells me as he carefully places a small bag into my outstretched hand. I speak with many exhibitors that day, but unfortunately cannot remember all this man says except for something about vermicastings, worms, and microbes. This interests me, as I'm beginning to awaken to the idea of living greener and more sustainably, but I don't yet make the connection or understand its greatness.

A year later my new friend Amanda invites me to dine al fresco in her backyard garden. Very creative, Amanda is a hip horticulturist who later authors *Kiss My Aster: A Graphic Guide to Creating a Fantastic Yard Totally Tailored to You,* and co-authors *Grocery Gardening.*

The Chicago Tribune features her on the cover of their Sunday Magazine with the headline *"Wild Flower: Amanda Thomsen Is Shaking Up What's Growing In Our Gardens."*

Amanda certainly shakes up what I grow in mine! A photograph pictures her standing in her garden, hands on her hips, a simple black sleeveless dress revealing a large tattoo of pruning shears on her upper arm. Vintage art deco-inspired Bakelite jewelry dangles from her neck and arms, and her platinum blond hair pulled back in a red bandana depict a Rosie the Riveter and Martha Stewart mash-up with a punk rock attitude thrown in!

We enjoy a delicious Caprese pizza with tomatoes and basil picked fresh from her garden, and I admire the lush landscape she's created and how healthy and vibrant her plants look. One thing puzzles me though: I don't see a vegetable garden, just a garden. She's cleverly integrated vegetable plants into the overall design. The result is stunning–and delicious!

"The secret," she confides to me, "is worm poop! C'mon" she then invites me, "lemme show you something!"

She stops at a table in her three-season room, just off her kitchen. She lifts the lid off of a black plastic tower made of stacked trays that resemble a pagoda, and instructs me to place some food scraps from our plates underneath the shredded newspaper on the top tray.

When she lifts the shredded newspaper, I see underneath huddled masses of squirming red worms! Awe is not my first impulse–rather it's more like disgust. A tomboy as a child, I baited my own hook when fishing, but thinking now about worms as inside-the-house cohabitants freaks me out a bit.

"Remember how I told you I use organic fertilizer?" Amanda asks. "Well, these guys are my secret weapon. They eat my garbage and transform it into black gold that plants love!"

Suddenly I remember the bag of alive soil, and it all begins to make sense! I'm not drawn to the idea of doing it myself, but understand why it's helpful to gardeners.

Inspired Into Action

"By the sweat of your brow will you have food to eat until you return to the ground from which you were made. For you were made from dust, and to dust you will return." ~ Genesis 3:19

Over the next several years I grow increasingly interested in the environment and decide I want to live more in harmony with nature. *Earth Day is great,* I muse, *but it's just once a year–I need more than that!* I begin to organize and host local monthly meetings called *Green Drinks* in order to help myself and others learn.

Green Drinks–held in 600-plus cities all over the world–attracts a lively mixture of people from academia, non-profit organizations, government entities, and the business world. I invite varied speakers to present brief lectures and provide a different focus each time.

I recruit a *Green Drinks* speaker to talk about permaculture–the philosophy that considers how plants and animals interact and that works with nature in a holistic manner, rather than designing a system around any single element.

Building soil is a vitally important aspect of permaculture. Modern intensive agricultural practices deplete the soil of nutrients. This results in the growing of fruits and vegetables that are not as nutritious as those grown decades ago.

Another aspect of permaculture is the concept of *guilds,* including plants that offer mutual support to one another. One example, drawn from Native American culture, is *the three sisters:* corn, beans, and squash. Tall, sturdy cornstalks support climbing bean tendrils. Beans draw nitrogen from the air and convert it into nutrients beneficial to squash and corn. Squash prevents weeds and keeps the soil moist and cool with its broad leaves.

The synergy of this system increases each plant's yield with fewer inputs than each requires if grown separately. I'm ready to start my own small-scale permaculture revolution! Time to find some worms!

My husband John graciously accepts our new housemates once I assure him they don't smell and will cause no problems. He gets used to using them as our "garbage disposal." It isn't long before the worms reward us with black gold and, after six months, we have about twenty gallons to use in our twelve by twelve-foot community vegetable garden plot.

I don't consider myself a green thumb, but this year our garden is wildly productive and stands out amongst the forty others. Another gardener friend notices the difference and asks if I'll show her how to start a worm compost bin.

After several others ask as well, I host a small workshop that ten people attend. Worms multiply rapidly if provided sufficient food stock, and I have plenty of worms to share!

Since this first workshop, I've conducted many more. In addition, I've spoken in front of church, college, and civic groups, now that I recognize the benefits of composting beyond mere gardening and soil conservation.

I become a certified Master Recycler and Composter in the first program of its kind in the state of Indiana, hosted by our county recycling and waste reduction district. The program's goal is to educate and empower a group of eco-conscious citizens to spread the word about what individuals can do to divert waste from landfills and keep our region's environment healthy.

Part of our educational experience consists of a visit to a landfill in the neighboring county of Newton, Indiana. One of the largest in the U.S., it appears well run. However, once the hundreds of acres that comprise the site are full to capacity, it will never again be suitable for farming, housing, or much else.

Tragically, much of the content destined to be sealed inside is comprised of compostable food waste and paper—worm food! Instead of black gold, this organic material will end up in a waste graveyard. This interruption of the natural cycle seems wrong in so many ways.

What a waste! I can't help thinking as I realize that one possible answer to many of our nutrition issues and landfill blight may just lie with the lowly earthworm!

Soothing Beyond Measure

"Grandfather, look at our brokenness. We know that in all creation, only the human family has strayed from the Sacred Way. We know that we are the ones who are divided, and we are the ones who must come back together to walk in the Sacred Way. Grandfather, Sacred One, teach us love, compassion, and honor. That we may heal the earth and heal each other." ~ Ojibway prayer

Etymology fascinates me. I learn that the root words *hum* and *human* both come from the Latin *humus*, meaning *earth and ground*, and the Latin *humanus* which means *man*, and I become deeply aware of the connection between my soil and me. The worms compost our dog's hair, dryer lint, and food scraps, and a little bit of our own DNA—I'm sure!—ends up in there somehow as well.

This rich compost yields nutritious vegetables that sustain our small household. The vegetable scraps return to the worm bin and return yet again to our garden as compost. The circle of life continues, and for some reason I find this soothing beyond measure.

My husband's quirky sense of humor takes a somewhat darker approach.

"If ever I go missing, check the worm bin!" he warns friends. Me? I think that would be a pretty good way to go—knowing I'll be returned to the circle of life in a meaningful way. Interdependent creatures, we need one another to survive. Grateful for this elegant lesson my worms teach me in a thousand small ways each and every day, I bless the beautiful "common ground" they produce.

My professional mission to help business people learn to harness the power of social media now includes adding all that I've learned about permaculture and eco-consciousness. Through all of my newfound knowledge I begin to bring gardening metaphors into my social media marketing consultant business.

In my training program *Finding Your Social Media DNA: Developing Naturally and Authentically,* I describe how one's garden thrives through healthy soil—even if one is not an expert gardener. Likewise, business success comes much more easily with a strong social network.

However, this does not necessarily require a huge investment of time in—or expertise about—sales and marketing! Clients can grow a healthy thriving business by applying the same eco-friendly mindset to identify common ground with their audiences and achieve— ultimately—nothing short of *transformational magic!*

ABOUT THE AUTHOR: Kathy is a fusion of business coach, storyteller, public speaker, tree hugger and marketing professional. Excited by the opportunity of social media for business, Sipple formed "My Social Media Coach" in 2009 with the mission of making social media marketing understandable and manageable for entrepreneurs and other small business owners. Kathy resides in Valparaiso, Indiana with her husband John and their black Lab, Bodhi. She holds a B.A. in Economics from the University of Michigan in Ann Arbor and is a member of Mensa. She is a reiki master/teacher, an avid hiker, nature photographer and community gardener.

Kathy Sipple
www.kathysipple.com
www.mysocialmediacoach.com

A Blessing In Disguise
Sharon Holand Gelfand

I watch helplessly as the blood drains from my twelve-and-a-half year-old son Zach's face and his hands clench slowly into fists. Suddenly his face turns beet red—as if ready to pop like a balloon—as he utters the most heartbreaking words I've ever heard him say.

"Am I going to *die?*"

"You're going to be fine," I say as I hug him tightly, but my heart sinks as I see him trying to process the information from the doctor—information that includes the word *disease.* "You're going to heal," I reassure him, though my stomach is in knots. For the first time in my life, I feel like I've lost control.

Zach's diagnosis comes in the middle of my divorce, and it's as though a storm has erupted and I've been sucked into a riptide and left gasping for air. There's a gaping hole in my life and I don't know how I'm ever going to make it through. What I *do know* is that I have to help my son.

"The medicine will help him, don't worry about changing his diet," the doctor tells me. She's not very supportive.

Zach's been diagnosed with inflammatory bowel disease (IBD), an autoimmune disorder (not to be confused with irritable bowel syndrome, or IBS) that involves chronic inflammation of all or part of the digestive tract and can include severe diarrhea, pain, fatigue, moodiness, and weight loss.

My gut reaction as a mom is to go online and research everything I can find about Crohn's disease, ulcerative colitis, and ileitis - all part of IBD.

How did I get to this point and what can I do to help my son? I wonder wearily. I feel as though I've become a spectator in own my life—watching from the sidelines. The past several years seem to have flashed by in a nanosecond...

All Figured Out

A first generation American, I'm raised to work hard, excel at what I do well, and always to do the right thing. Don't ask questions, do what you are told, and stop dreaming—it doesn't pay the bills!

Don't get me wrong, I love my parents, but this is the belief system I learn based on their doing the best job they can with the tools they possess. I never question my path, which I understand is to work hard and not complain, get married, have kids, save money, and gain security. Then I'll be all set.

I have it all figured out at an early age. In my mind I paint a picture of what my future should look like, and always I maintain control. I happen to be good with numbers, so I become a commercial banker.

Everything is black and white to a banker. After all, numbers are numbers—one plus one will always equal two. I live my life this way for a long time. Since everything is always linear, so are my expectations and assumptions.

By the time I marry and have kids, I *think* my life is under control, yet I've become hypoglycemic, anemic, experience chronic migraines, eczema, mood swings, digestive issues, and more. Still I consider myself healthy. Besides, my doctor says that my symptoms are common—given the stress of family, work and life—and that I shouldn't worry about them.

He tells me to take iron for my anemia and Imitrex shots for my migraines, and sends me on my way. I share this with my friends, many of whom experience the same ailments, and simply accept that that there's nothing I can do about it. Or so I think...

Coming Into Focus

My internet research—in the hope of helping Zach—leads me consistently to the topic of nutrition and its impact on the body and mind. The more I learn, the more passionate I become about the subject, but also the more confusing the information seems. I don't know who or what to believe!

The banker in me analyzes everything and I consult with friends who are health coaches—but still there are so many questions left unanswered. I realize *I* need to be the expert—to go from misinformed to properly informed—and I decide to go back to graduate school to obtain a master's degree in clinical nutrition.

In the course of my studies I discover that everything I've heard on the radio and in television advertisements, *and* what I've read in magazines and on food boxes, is *all wrong!* I don't want to believe that companies would lie to me about their food products, so I've never questioned any of it—until now. I realize that all this time I've been walking around mindless and asleep!

Previously, I *thought* I was eating healthy, but now the more I prepare and feed my family whole, real, unprocessed food, the healthier my son gets and the healthier I become. So consumed with helping Zach, I haven't thought about my own issues with health or weight. Soon *every* symptom—gone! To top it off, I have more energy than since before my first son was born! Not only has my body changed for the better, I've actually lost weight!

Now I stand in my closet, staring at my dark blue jeans hanging on a yellow hanger.

Try me on—I dare you, try me! they tease. My heart races. Dare I try on my tight jeans?

Slowly I reach for the hanger and pull them off. I sit down on the bed and begin to put one leg in, but stop midway at the knee. I think for a split second of taking them off and putting them back in the closet, where they belong.

Go for it! a voice inside says, so I do. In slides my other leg and slowly I stand up. I pull up my pants, all the while holding my breath.

Whew, they fit over my hips! Now I've got them up to my waist! The final test is to see if they'll close. The zipper glides up easily. I stand there, shocked! I can't remember the last time I've worn these "just in case" jeans—kept in my closet "just in case" I'd ever fit into them again!

From that moment on and every day after, they become the jeans that just fit, always.

Shifting Into Mindfulness

It isn't until I put on these jeans and realize that they fit, that I ask myself: *how did this happen? I'm not on a diet—in fact, I'm eating more—and I've achieved this weight loss without dieting, depriving myself, counting calories, points ,or anything else!*

Suddenly, I make the connection—it's the *types* of food with which I'm nourishing my body! They're real whole foods, not processed or "fake" products. What a major shift in my relationship with food!

It's truly amazing how you don't know what you don't know, yet as soon as a little light is let in your perspective changes. It's like peering through a dirty window through which everything looks fuzzy. However, the view changes when you spray window cleaner on the cloudy muck and wipe it with a clean cloth.

All of a sudden, you see blooming trees and the clear azure blue sky! You clean a little more, and soon the whole backyard comes into focus and you notice it's sunny and birds are flying in a V-formation in the sky. You never want that window to be dirty again because you enjoy that tranquil view—it makes you smile!

Despite my lifetime history of dieting and chronic health issues, as I made small steady shifts with food choices and lifestyle, my body—and Zach's—began the healing process. What starts out as a quest to conquer and heal my son's condition turns into a rise in my own consciousness, which is life-changing and transformational.

The surprising part is that the healing comes through food itself—eating healthy food heals the body *and* nourishes the soul. Providing my body with the right nutrients helps eliminate my brain fog and other symptoms. In addition to thinking more clearly, I notice that I'm happier and feel somehow lighter.

This, in turn, gives me space to think more clearly and to feel more connected—to my kids, family, and friends. They see these changes and comment not only on my increased energy but also on how I seem more at peace.

One day, as I read through a journal in which I began writing at the beginning of this journey, I realize how drastically my level of consciousness has shifted and how I no longer feel the need to always be in control. Zach's diagnosis teaches me that we all have a choice. Life happens. Curve balls are thrown at us constantly, but it's *how* we react to a situation that helps us grow and make a difference.

When faced with Zach's health issues, I made a conscious decision to take action. Like Neo in *The Matrix,* I've taken the red pill. I've shifted into mindfulness in every aspect of my life as a veil has been lifted. No longer am I on autopilot—the pieces of the puzzle all fall into place. Instead of feeling the need to be in control and to always plan for the future, I've found the room to let go and *be present.*

Filled with gratitude, I wonder *without health, what do we have really?* The importance of this question became apparent to me upon hearing Zach's diagnosis. If we're not one hundred percent healthy, how can we live fully? If we're not nourishing our physical bodies and our souls, how can we possibly be present to give energy, love, or light to anyone around us?

Suddenly I have an epiphany: *if I didn't know this...who else doesn't know it? Who else is sleepwalking, waiting to feel great, and do something extraordinary with their life?*

And that's when I realize I have to help people! My personal transformation which has been life-changing in so many ways, ultimately leads me to help women connect to their bodies and learn to live consciously through nutritional coaching.

My journey down the nutrition path begins with window cleaning, but ends up with soul cleansing. Given an opportunity and a second lease on life, it's one I'd never have found on my own. It's my son's diagnosis that shifts everything—what a blessing in disguise!

ABOUT THE AUTHOR: A clinical nutritionist, lifestyle & nutritional designer, speaker, and author, Sharon holds a Master's in clinical nutrition and works with individual clients to "feducate" them to find balance and freedom from the constraints of traditional dieting. Infused with real life insight and inspiration, her unique perspective on nutrition empowers her clients to eat more and lose weight, while taking ownership of their food choices. Whether it's about losing weight, low energy, brain fog, or Type II Diabetes, Sharon provides the tools to give her clients their health and their lives back, and helps them create their own roadmap to good health!

Sharon Holand Gelfand
www.sharonholand.com
sharon@tierrasol.com
www.facebook.com/tierrasollife

PART TWO

Conscious Relationships

"The most powerful tool that I can share with you to transform any situation is the power of blessing with love."
~ Cheryl Richardson

Breathing In Life
Deborah Tray

I wish these dolphins would simply take me away, I muse, as I float in the beautiful water off Sanibel Island, Florida. I ponder how I have given up on life and simply don't care anymore. I would almost welcome a cancer diagnosis as a result of my recent pap smear, so tired am I of fighting to be happy. My children grown, I don't feel I have a reason to go on—*I'm tired of my unhappy, depressing life.*

It's in these beautiful warm waters while on vacation that I come to a crossroads in my life. Do I stay or do I go? *How easy it would be to simply start swimming and let the dolphins take care of me as I let myself slip away...so tempting, so inviting...*

In this moment I know I can't do it—I can't leave this earth without fulfilling my purpose. I can't die with my life's music still in me unsung. I must know what life can be like when I am at peace, blissfully enjoying *truly* living...

Dear God, I pray, *help me to no longer be in pain, emotionally and physically. Help me to live a life where I experience happiness and peace daily.* And here, on this warm day in the crystal clear blue waters of southwest Florida, I vow to heal my life and honor myself by embracing the many blessings I know lie waiting for me to claim.

I'd like to say everything changed the instant I stepped out of the water, but this is only the beginning of the next chapter of my lifelong journey of healing—emotionally, spiritually, and physically. As I learn to release old patterns, my life begins to unravel—and only then do I start to build a new, stronger foundation...

Re-Alignment

I return home from vacation to learn that my test results show abnormal cell growth, but no cancer. The pain from my period is excruciating and lasts for two weeks at a time, often accompanied by debilitating migraine headaches.

I undergo a surgical procedure intended to stop my period and this relieves me of my pain and discomfort. I begin to realize that although I've studied healing extensively for more than twenty years and meditate daily, I never fully trust in the guidance I'm given. I'm too ensconced in letting my ego rule my life. It's taken until menopause seriously affects my health for me to admit what I feel in my heart: *I haven't been living a life aligned with my true core values.* I know now I have to make the necessary changes I've put off for far too long. My marriage to Tom, on life support for years—we'd rally, have some good times, and then fall back into the same old patterns of barely existing together—is destroying us both.

We married young, didn't know how to communicate our feelings, thoughts, and desires, and eventually we shut down. I know Tom has it in him to be nurturing, kind, and gentle, but he simply can't show it. He drinks and becomes caustic, and in turn, I become depressed, sad, lonely, and despondent.

The stark reality of my situation hits me when—while nursing my cat Holly during the three weeks leading to her passing—I feel more love and appreciation from this little black cat who is dying than I have from Tom in years. Suddenly I realize: *Oh my God, I can't go on like this...*

Christmas approaches and I sense this will be our last holiday together as a family. Honestly, I have no more to give this relationship. Only fear of the unknown is keeping me from moving on with my life. A few months later, just shy of our twenty-ninth wedding anniversary, I tell Tom I am leaving.

A New Chapter

The day before our divorce is finalized, I see Tom one last time to sign some paperwork. I begin to sob as I start to leave. He hugs me as I tell him how sorry I am that we were not kinder and more loving to each other. This is one of the most tender and loving moments of our marriage. How sad that we handled our divorce with more love and respect than we did our marriage!

I ponder how things might have been different had we been honest with our feelings. Trying to forgive myself is difficult—I feel responsible for not doing enough for him, for *us*. I punish myself by holding onto my transgressions, my failures. However, I begin to learn that even in my darkest moments, God won't give up on me—I must simply be open to receiving His divine love and guidance.

I move into a cozy cottage on the outskirts of Nashville, Tennessee, where a friend has recently relocated. What a difference from living in an upper middle class neighborhood in Houston, Texas! The cottage seems to enfold me with love and protection, and it's here I begin to rest, heal, and unravel and understand my life.

I rediscover my core values of integrity, self-respect, and trust in the power of love, and to align my life with them. I realize forgiving Tom is necessary if I want to achieve the peace that has eluded me. Not only must I forgive Tom, but it is imperative that I forgive myself, which does not come easily. I learn to peel back layers and continually go through the process of tearing down old beliefs and building anew as my healing unfolds.

Shortly after arriving in Nashville I reconnect with Don, my college sweetheart who is also newly divorced. Don and I had spoken a few times during my long marriage, and I never forgot the love, kindness, and caring he showed me so many years ago.

In Nashville on his way to a job in New Orleans, he asks to meet me. We meet and, as we stand up at the end of our conversation, he reaches for my hand. I know we both recognize the feelings still in our hearts for each other.

If I take this man's hand, my life will change forever, I think, and know I have a choice to make. I decide not to let any more time go by without exploring what this relationship might become. *I don't want to wait another thirty years!*

Don relocates to Nashville, and another chapter of my new life journey begins.

No Going Back

As Don and I heal from our former marriages, I learn to trust in love and our relationship. As time passes I find my voice, speak my truth, and learn to honor and respect myself. I start to become the woman I'd long since forgotten, and to embrace her.

When Don proposes to me in a sweet and sentimental way at our church two years from the day we reconnected, I'm excited to marry again! However, shortly after, the same menopausal pain resurfaces. Doubled over, once again I submit to testing—only to find it's my body reacting to the menopausal changes I'm going through. I know it's a clear message that getting married is not in God's plan for us at this time. The pain subsides...

I remain behind when Don moves back to Pennsylvania to restart his business there, since it never quite materialized in Nashville. We begin a long distance relationship for the next fifteen months and, during this separation, I use the time to delve deeper into learning to love and forgive myself. I know I must take this challenging journey to achieve the peace for which I so long.

Along the way I meet a group of wonderful women who help me to know God, and to believe He placed me on this earth to fulfill a divine purpose. I read constantly, listen to spiritual and inspirational teachers, and practice what I am learning as I embrace my calling as a life coach and Reiki healing practitioner.

As I prepare to join Don in Pennsylvania, I sit sorting through pictures and letters from my past and begin to relive all of the old pain from my marriage—and with it returns my feelings of guilt, shame, and blame. I'd struggled for years with asthma, and suddenly I feel my lungs closing up and realize I'm in serious trouble.

Dear Jesus, I can't do this to myself again—please help me! I grab my nebulizer but can't breathe enough to fill it. I struggle to reach the phone and dial 911 for help—I know I can't get to the hospital on my own. The medics arrive in an ambulance to take me the three short miles to the hospital. Later, I'm told I had no breath sounds and needed to be stabilized when they started working on me.

Afterward, I realize I've taken a huge step backward by journeying again to that dark place where I blame myself and my ex-husband. How could I work so hard to heal, but then allow myself to walk right back into the nightmare of feeling undeserving of happiness?

The old pain of not forgiving myself shut me down—literally took my breath away! In that moment I learn that going back to a past I regret is never the answer. It's merely the ego's way of keeping us in chains, bound to the past.

As I close the door to my cottage for the final time, I know I have a whole glorious life ahead of me with the man I love in a new home. So much to live for, including teaching, coaching, and helping others heal *their* lives. I marvel now at the courage it took for me to make the journey out of darkness and into a place of peace, and how—now that I've opened my heart to love and forgiveness—I'm breathing in life's joy, peace, and blessings...

ABOUT THE AUTHOR: At a young age Deborah heard the verse, "Let there be peace on earth and let it begin with me." These words so moved her, she knew her life's calling was to help others achieve peace and healing in their life. Deborah is a Certified Holistic Life

Coach with a Bachelor's degree in Social Work, whose mission is to support women on their journey to heal and grow spiritually, emotionally, mentally, and physically. Deborah is a powerful energy healer, incorporating the use of Reiki, Qigong and meditation to further bring healing and wholeness to her clients.

Deborah Tray, CPC, ELI-MP
www.deborahtraycoaching.com
deborahtraycoaching@gmail.com
www.deborahtray.juiceplus.com
215-767-7163

A Sister's Soul Contract:
Death, Healing, & Transformation
Christina Ann Sullivan

"Christina!"

I hear the panic in my mother's voice on the other end of the phone.

"The paramedics were at Kathy's house—they tried to resuscitate her and now she's in an ambulance on the way to the hospital!"

"I'll be right home," I tell Mom calmly even though my heart's in my throat. I don't want her to hear any terror in my voice.

I hang up the phone and run to the bathroom as my heart sinks to my stomach. Fear rises to the surface and I let out a scream. These phone calls about my sister are not all that unfamiliar—she's had many similar incidents in and out of the hospital over the years, but always manages to pull through. Somehow I always know she will. This time I feel differently, but desperately try to deny that I know this time is the final one.

The door to the bathroom flies open as my coworkers run in to see who's screamed. On the floor in a heap shaking and crying, I'm almost unable to get myself together as they console me. I gather my belongings—completely distraught as all manner of fearful thoughts race through my mind.

My mom's only just lost her own mother eight months prior and is still grieving. My coworker and friend Amber takes my keys to drive my car while another colleague follows, which allows me time to get myself together. I need to be strong for my mom.

"Everything's going to be alright, it always is with your sister," Amber tries to reassure me. She hugs me as she walks me to my door, which I dread opening because I know on the other side my mother is a wreck.

"If we hurry we can make Tampa in five hours!" Mom's in a panic, packing frantically as my girlfriend—with whom I've been living for the past several years—is on the computer checking for flights in the hope of getting us there sooner. The phone rings and my heart almost stops.

"She's gone—Kathy's gone!" cries my brother. In that one sentence I feel like a thousand knives are plunged into my chest and someone has reached inside of me and ripped out my heart. I let out a scream that sounds like something from a horror movie—no surprise as this is my real life horror.

My sister is dead! I'll never see her again and I didn't even get to say good-bye! Upon hearing me scream my mother runs into the bedroom where I'm standing crying.

"No Christina, not my Kathy!" she wails and grabs her chest with her left hand as her right hand reaches out.

"Mommy, mommy, mommy!" she suddenly begins to repeat nonstop.

My heart races as I wonder if she's seeing her own deceased mother, or possibly having a heart attack.

"Call nine-one-one!" I yell to my girlfriend, as I place my mother on a chair, and look directly into her glazed-over eyes. Unresponsive to my questions, she doesn't seem coherent.

"God help my mother!" I say out loud in sheer panic. "I just lost my sister, please help!"

I begin to pray and in that moment—as I'm kneeling on the floor holding my mom—she begins to rock me gently. Then she speaks:

"Chris," she says, "everything's going to be alright." What's going on? My mother never calls me Chris! "I'm always going to be with you both! Don't be sad..."

Little do I realize in this moment that this is not good-bye at all for my sister Kathy and me. With all the fear I have around my mother's health, it clouds my awareness to what's actually occurring right before my eyes...Kathy is speaking through Mom!

The paramedics arrive, check my mother's vitals, and tell us she's completely fine—just in a state of shock, as are we all. Life as we know it will never be the same.

"Death Ends A Life, Not A Relationship." ~ Robert Benchley

My three siblings all have the same father, the man to whom my mother was married for twenty years right out of high school. I am the product of an affair. Led to believe that my siblings' father is the same as mine, as far back as I can remember I have an inner knowing that I'm somehow different.

Always I have the unsettled feeling that I do not belong in my family. None of my siblings make me feel this way, but because of the rather obvious differences in skin tone and features—they are full Irish and I'm half Sicilian—it creates conflict within me at a very early age.

Unhappy in her marriage, my mom separates from her husband and moves in with my biological father. I'm raised very differently from my siblings, as my father is violent and physically abuses my mom and me throughout my childhood.

Thank God for my sister Kathy who always comes to rescue me from the nightmare and bring me into a magical dream. I'm the youngest and she's the eldest—there are eighteen years between us— and because our birthdays are a week apart we always celebrate them together. My mom tells me how Kathy used to stare at me in my bassinet for hours and say I'd be the most beautiful of all—the first sign of our unique connection and soul bond.

Extremely protective and motherly toward me, Kathy loves to have fun, possesses an infectious laugh, and is completely selfless. She loves to travel, and takes me many places, including amusement parks, plays, movies, and my very first rock concert!

When I become an adult, Kathy's not only my sister but my confidante and best friend. There isn't anything I can't confide to her and she's always supportive of me whenever I need her. A juvenile diabetic, Kathy endures many health issues, and over the years suffers two strokes and a heart attack. A survivor, she overcomes every health crisis, which often leaves her doctors in a state of wonderment. Whenever she's hospitalized I'm right by her bedside.

On many occasions the doctors think she may not survive. I pray so hard for her to stay with me—I don't feel I can make it through life without her! No matter where I live or work, when Kathy's in the hospital I'm there. I leave everything to be with her, and stay until I know she's well.

"A Sister Is A Gift To The Heart, A Friend To The Spirit, A Golden Thread To The Meaning Of Life." ~ Isadora James

When Kathy dies I switch to survival mode—my natural state during childhood. I have to be strong for my mother, make all the funeral arrangements, and hold her and everyone up, when all I want to do is fall apart. I maintain my strength through the services and until I settle back into my life. Then my emotions come bearing down on me like a hailstorm during a hurricane.

My own destructive force most of my life, I used drugs and alcohol as ways to escape—especially when dealing with feelings of pain. Now in such pain and agony over the unbearable loss of Kathy, all I want to do is drown myself in a bottle.

Angry with myself for not making it to see Kathy in the hospital before she died makes this idea very tempting—what a great way to numb out and punish myself for being such a horrible sister! Somehow—as tempting as it is—I find a greater resolve within myself and refuse to give in to this destructive pattern. This becomes a major turning point.

God works in synchronistic ways. A few months before Kathy's death I'm introduced to Reiki, truly a blessing in my life! I attribute my ability to endure my sister's death and to overcome my self-destructive patterns and behaviors to these Reiki healing sessions. Not quite conscious of it at that time, I understand later that healing had begun on all levels—mental, emotional, spiritual, and physical.

Many challenges and adversarial forces confront me all at once soon after my sister's death. Within weeks of my loss, I'm fired from my job and my girlfriend breaks up with me and moves out.

Working as a restaurant server/manager, I earned a great income and was very comfortable in my job. I'm angry with my boss for betraying me in this way—especially after just losing my sister—given all my dedicated years of service. However, getting fired enables me to collect unemployment and provides me the room I so desperately need to grieve.

As for my relationship, we weren't on the greatest of terms anyway. I stayed, even though it was clearly no longer working. These betrayals by others only reflected how I was betraying myself.

Do all of these events occurring in my life serve my higher purpose? I wonder. I realize it's a matter of my perception. I choose to view them both as blessings in disguise. If I hadn't gotten fired I'd probably never have left. And the loss of my girlfriend pales in comparison to the loss of my sister—I'm still breathing, life goes on, and I'll meet someone new, but I'll never physically see my sister again.

During this time I know I have to allow myself room to feel my emotions. I choose to journal, and through this process my sister Kathy comes to me. I start receiving messages from her through automatic handwriting, and it's then that it hits me—our relationship isn't over, it's simply changed form!

The skeptic in me finds this hard to believe and leads me on a journey to seek out psychics, healers, and spiritual advisors. Happily, I find confirmation and validation of what I'm experiencing, and come to learn about my own psychic gifts and healing abilities. My sister's death is the catalyst to my great awakening!

I know that—with so many wounds to heal—the healing ultimately must begin with me. There's so much conditioning and programming to undo within that I decide to work with the best of healers and coaches and engage in many different healing modalities.

In honor of myself and my sister—and with gratitude in my heart for my connection with Kathy—I embark on my path of healing. I learn to take responsibility for my own life, and realize that everything in my external world is merely a reflection of my inner one. I can't change anyone—I can only change myself—and when I heal it inevitably affects everyone in my life.

I discover my purpose is to be of service to all those seeking transformation, and that the greatest gift I can ever give myself is my own healing transformation—the kind forged through death and a sister's soul contract.

ABOUT THE AUTHOR: Christina Ann Sullivan, a Denise Linn Certified Soul Coach® & Past life regression facilitator, Certified Usui Shiki RYoho Reiki Master, Certified Akashic Record reader, and Advanced Certified Medicinal Aromatherapist, dedicates her career to helping people heal on all levels—spiritual, mental, emotional, and physical. Passionate about being of service, Christina shares the ideas and practices that helped her most, including how to access one's inner intuitive wisdom to awaken into soul consciousness and trust that all answers lie within. Inspired by her sister, Christina created *Kathy's Lifeflow* to help clients heal, revitalize, and bring balance to mind, body, and spirit.

Christina Ann Sullivan
954-732-3104
www.Kathyslifeflow.com

Never Settle Again
Morgan Sontag

The tendonitis in my right elbow screams and my body aches. Schlepping heavy building materials has taken its toll on my small frame after one too many trips to Home Depot. It's Sunday night at closing time—another weekend eaten up by never-ending projects, most of which are not my own.

"No, I don't want to do this!" I'd say—*sometimes*. But often I'd hold back, weighing the consequences. Would it be worth the predictable argument?

"Well, you never want to go!" my partner counters. "This is what's required to be a good partner. In relationship, supportive means you help out. And when all this is finished, you'll be happy."

Stop complaining, I'd scold myself, *you signed on for this.* Clearly, I have not mastered the art of compromise or how to stand firm when it comes to Home Depot runs.

Clutter free in 2003! I write on the living room wall sheetrock. But the chaos continues into 2004, 2005, and 2006! Camping in a slogged down, do-it-yourself remodel, I feel victimized by circumstances outside my control, or so it seems. Washing dishes in the bathroom sink gets old fast. This is not the first time I've gone along with a partner's dream, unclear and/or unsure of my own.

So here I am at Home Depot, resources and stamina running dry, nerves on end, in a relationship filled with stress and disorganization. I can't figure out a solution to stop the domino effect of cumulating challenges. Disempowered and hopeless, I exist with imaginary ropes around my wrists.

And when I'm not in victim position, I'm pissed, self-critical, or blaming. *How did I get myself into this mess? What the hell was I thinking or, worse yet—not thinking? I'm smart,* I badger myself, *so surely I can figure this out!* Then I shift to become the villain, and ramp up the blame. Eventually, I step into fix-it mode and hero, or remedy the situation by cooking a nice meal and reassuring myself *it will all turn out ok*. Around and around I'd go, from victim to villain to hero, spinning in these three positions, never solving a thing, merely changing seats on the Titanic.

Pickled In A Legacy

My parents, both teachers, move from northern California to a small conservative Washington state town where rules exist for how to behave to keep gossip at bay. If a boy asks me out, I have to go.

"You don't want to hurt his feelings, or be a snob," Mom insists. Like eating Brussels sprouts, *give it a try*. This rule also means *try it more than once—you might change your mind*.

"Be thankful for the opportunity, and that somebody asked you out," Dad always chimes in. "And if he wants to kiss you goodnight, go along with it! Be polite! It might upset his parents or they'll think we don't approve!"

Shit, these boys will never get to first base, I'd think defiantly. *And I hate Brussels sprouts!* Yet I don't realize how these values seep insidiously into my own habits and viewpoints. So sneaky, and soon I find myself in college repeating history, obliging no matter who asks me out. *Try it, you might like it.*

"To be in a relationship is better than being alone," Mom says repeatedly. Pickled in a legacy of compliant women who settled for less, her advice to my various relationship dilemmas is of no help. Eventually, I date women too. Same script...*go ahead and try it*. Gender is irrelevant. If I agree to date past the first outing, our time and energy is often dominated by my partner's preference.

"I've seen that movie already!" I might protest.

"You can see it again, can't you?" is the reply, "because *I* want to go!" *Keep the peace. It won't hurt. Behave yourself. Learn to cooperate.*

Don't misunderstand me, I'm no wall-flower or push-over. In fact, in many ways I play the leader, instigator, or infiltrator. A rebel who never gets caught, I'm split—I succeed at being a great student, and philosopher, but behind the scenes I'm wild, racing and on a spiritual quest.

An outspoken, opinionated, dominating spit-fire, I debate with the best, especially in class. I concoct many wild-ass adventures, and enroll lovers and friends on numerous escapades. Hell-bent on exploring, learning, expanding my consciousness through meditation and spirituality while bending unfair rules, questioning authority, picketing, protesting, and speaking out, I'm nevertheless scared of anger, though I house a seething cauldron down below.

"There's no way I'll have surgery to be joined at the hip!" I argue and philosophize with my college pals."Why can't a relationship be supportive of one another's dreams, and allow each person to grow and evolve in separate and connected ways? Can't a relationship be the icing on the top and not the ultimate goal?"

"You're nuts, nobody will go for that!" my friends retort. "You must be scared of commitment, or maybe you're non-monogamous. You're crazy! Nobody will marry you! If you want to go to school in New York while your husband works in San Diego, it will never happen!" I stop talking about alternatives.

I am a walking dichotomy—outspoken and a leader, but driven to avoid conflict. As my own little watch-dog, I sniff out any inkling of attack and take up my defensive guns. Not rocking the boat provides a safe, usually quiet alternative—my personal favorite. I see that codependency and pleasing others pays off. Any hint of big anger or conflict and my specialties become skirting an issue, deflecting, giving in, disappearing, or going silent. If my first arsenal of tactics fails to stop or divert an argument, I roll out my cannon and blast away. Overall, it's best to keep an even tone through my gritted smile and accommodate over and over—because keeping the peace is a prize.

The Conscious Heart

This can't be what I'm supposed to be doing—where is my life? I implore the universe on my daily solitary walks. *Please show me the way!* becomes my mantra as I look to the sky with outstretched arms.

Working as a counselor in private practice, I lack enthusiasm. Uninspired and bored, I need a change. It seems a random act when I begin to read *The Conscious Heart* by Gay and Kathlyn Hendricks, whose whole-body collaborative approach to addressing challenges is provocative and inspiring. What's in the body running underground? How do you access, consciously heal, and release old patterns and limiting beliefs through your body?

I google the Hendricks, and three months later fly to meet them. I enroll in a two-year apprenticeship that literally unzips the layers I can't strip away on my own—even though I'm a "shrink" myself.

I love their approach, which basically is about living and communicating authentically, and not settling for less than what I truly want in life. I jump in full throttle. While learning and expanding, I remain baffled and challenged in my home environment. My work shifts from counseling to coaching, which makes a huge difference. Lighter and more hopeful after an exhilarating day, I'd go home and face the incongruence of living in a stuck zone. *Does coaching about possibilities while remaining personally out of alignment leave me too entrenched in my history and habits to rectify my situation?* I wonder.

One Saturday afternoon I've had enough—enough of the challenges, disappointments, cyclic arguing, hauling of lumber, rocks, furniture—simply *enough!* Tired of loyalty at all costs, of not prioritizing me, of losing myself, giving myself away, settling big time in various jobs and relationships, mastering the victim position—*poor me!*—enough is enough. I plead with source energy to guide me, and vow to take myself on.

Suddenly I feel a palpable *clunk!* in my body. Unmistakably a full-body *no!* it's as if I've landed. Clearly it's *over*, and I won't settle for one more minute! As I land in my body, I get out of my head and into my full self...

This revelation delivers a sudden surge of energy and excitement, but also a twinge of fear. I know undeniably the time has arrived for me to fully emerge and prioritize my heart and soul's work, my desires, and my life. No more settling for less than what I truly want. No more slipping into silence to avoid conflict. No more blame, complaint, and conflict. No more *yes's* when I feel *no*—no more Brussels sprouts! I have no idea what's ahead, only that I won't be compromising myself any more.

I realize also that if I don't rotor-rooter out some outdated lurking beliefs and get down to some core doo-doo, I'm likely to recreate another version of my history. Determined to get to the bottom of what I set up and created unconsciously, I pull in my focus. I pay attention. On alert, benignly vigilant, I stop the old thoughts which no longer work. I interrupt my self-criticism, shift my thinking, name my positive gifts and talents, and focus on gratitude. I identify the bullshit and begin to tell the truth. Do I really have all of these deficits and flaws?

Slowly the fog lifts and it becomes apparent that I'm in charge of my experiences and my results. This is all an inside job, and has little to do with the story happening outside of me. Learning how to source my own self-respect, self-worth, and love is key. I stop seeking others' approval and spackling the cracks around my heart and mind with distractions, people, experiences. I simply stop all of the automatic ways in which I engage with others to avoid being with myself. I stop and feel my feelings as they arise.

I locate where in my body I feel the sensations, and notice my memories. I stop listening to my mental chatter—the voices of the critic, judge, comparer, blamer, victim, skeptic, doubter, and the not-good-enough natterer. These are habits of thought with attached beliefs that are all up for grabs now. None of them are actually true, or even make sense—they're nothing more than snippets of thought stitched together to grapple with confusing childhood scenarios, scary conflicts, and overwhelming feelings.

Now I begin to learn how to have an uncompromising relationship with myself. I learn to listen fully, express truth, and release my rigid defense system. I make a long list of people I want to forgive. Forgiving myself is at the top. I let go. In the meantime, I coach rather than counsel others in the Hendricks full-body learning style. This means there's far less time spent regurgitating problems, and I focus instead on what's happening—and held—in the body, which illuminates mythology and informs wiser choices in the present.

I wake up every morning now streaming joy, no matter what's on the agenda. And while shit happens, it has no clout because I am free, open, expanded, and exuberantly happy. I *know* I'll never settle again...

ABOUT THE AUTHOR: "Resolving issues doesn't have to be hard!" says Morgan Sontag, M.S., *Break Free* to an extraordinary life coach, psychotherapist, educator, trainer, catalyst, and Hendricks Institute Transformational Leaders Program graduate. Morgan specializes in employing cutting-edge approaches that help dissolve negative mental patterns—criticizing, defending, denying, withholding, etc.—which prevent full self-expression. Weaving quick-witted humor with fun, Morgan guides clients to expand their capacity for joy by opening "stuck" places to unleash freedom and hidden potential. Daily doses of tear-streaming laughter, surprises, theater, traveling, meeting people, and learning as much as possible keep life fresh and enlivening for Morgan.

Morgan Sontag, MS
Break Free Therapy & Coaching
www.breakfreetherapy.com
morgan@breakfreetherapy.com
206-940-6965

Precious Child
Brenda Fedorchuk

Lights flash, machines beep—tubes are attached to every part of her body. The doctor places his hand on my left shoulder and says "she cannot survive this, she has one-hundred percent mortality—the life-support machines are all that's keeping her alive."

Oh God! I panic. *This is not good!* I can't breathe, my heart pounds loudly in my head, and tears well up as I look into the eyes of my brother and sister, both standing beside me. Though no words pass between us, instinctively I know we all agree: *this can't be how it ends!*

Behind walls I'd put up to protect myself long ago my heart feels such deep sadness. I pray silently and ask for guidance. *What is it I need to know to be of the highest service in this moment?*

Looking at Mom, suddenly I feel a compassion I've never known before. I understand that she lived her life to the best of her ability. I know she'd be terrified to face what lies ahead. I remember as a child how frightened she could be, often feeling too afraid to drive alone—always needing someone to accompany her.

Instantly, I know this isn't about me. All the work I've done to heal—every bit of my self-help journey—has led me to this moment. It's no longer about the difficulties that have come between us, the life we did not share, the support I never had, the grandchildren she did not know. This is about rising above my "stuff" to courageously stand beside her as they remove the machines so that her life here on earth can end.

The Responsible One

"Mom, wake up!"

No response.

"Mom, wake up, you need to sign my report card! The teacher

said I have to hand it in to her today—I can't be late with it again!"

I'm nine. Every morning I get myself and my siblings off to school. Mom sleeps till noon, unable to get out of bed until she takes her *nerve pills*. We move around a lot. In fourth grade we move four times.

Although my stepfather's a hard worker, he's also an alcoholic who has to support four children from his first marriage. This doesn't leave much to support us. Many times I beg my mom for money so I can go to the corner store and buy something for supper. Often, she pulls out fifty cents and I run to buy bologna.

I hate her *nerve pills*. Never the same after she starts taking them, my mother's in a constant zombie-like state, emotionally unavailable. She can't clean the house or look after my baby sister. I have to go to school, come home, and be the responsible one because I'm the eldest.

At age ten I'm drawn to the church. I get up on Sunday mornings, walk about a mile to the nearest church by myself, and sit in the pew alone. No one notices me. I'm invisible.

One Christmas when I'm twelve my brothers receive this big wonderful stereo, and all I get for a present is a diary. I cry over the blatant inequity.

"Oh, grow up," my mother says condescendingly. "You're the oldest, you need to understand" she admonishes me, dismissing my feelings. The only thing I understand is that this is more proof she doesn't love me!

I know instinctively I can't count on Mom for anything. I'm convinced, as the eldest child, that I must protect my brothers and sister so they don't experience the same. I believe there's something deeply wrong with me. I put up a good front, but surely if folks knew, they'd believe I was a terrible, unlovable person. Why else would a mother treat her daughter like this?

If my mother becomes angry, her energy returns and she's a force to be reckoned with. She seeks revenge and holds a grudge at all costs. Often she yells and screams at me.

"Who do you think you are?" she says as she cuts me down to size. "You're getting too big for your britches!" She tells me how someday I'll need those nerve pills too!

Oh no, you're wrong—not me! a little voice inside me says. *I'll never take those pills...this is not going to be my life! I'm going to make something out of my life, wait and see!*

Making Something Of Myself

Turns out that the diary opens up to me a world previously unknown. I find journaling to be comforting—my own safe world into which I can retreat. *Dear God,* I start my journal every day. I write to tell Him all the terrible things that have happened to me, and to plead with Him to release me from my pain and misery.

I begin to work at fifteen as a means of escaping my household, and from that day forward I pay for everything I need, including my first car. I come home from work one day to find we've been locked out of the house. My books are inside and I have a twelfth grade final the next day.

My stepfather's drinking escalates, and I move out for a while. I don't do well in school that year. I'm so ashamed—none of these things happen at my friend's homes, and I envy their seemingly perfect lives. I vow never to find myself in this situation when I grow up.

A strong student, but with no opportunity to attend university—especially since my marks hit an all-time low during my twelfth grade year—I watch as my friends plan their future educations. The more they speak of their hopes and dreams, the more hopeless I feel, stuck with no one to help me, no one to turn to, no one in whom to confide.

My grandfather Walter and Uncle Ken understand—they're my silent supporters. If they dare get involved it only becomes worse for me. Grandfather Walter advises me to leave my house as soon as I can manage to be on my own. He reads tarot cards and sends me to a local tea leaf reader for guidance. He opens up the desire in me to learn more about forces unseen and unheard. Believing that there must be a better way, I read everything on Greek gods, mythology, horoscopes, and wonder what it's all about...

At seventeen I move away to the city. I have no money but know how to work hard. I find a number of odd jobs to pay my bills. I land a job as a photographer at eighteen and travel the country. I love it, am good at it, and get paid well. I'm even offered a job with a rock music magazine to take photos and interview rock bands!

Eventually, however, the travel becomes burdensome and I want something with more stability and income I can count on. Luckily I land a job in the corporate government world with a regular paycheck, benefits, and security—even though I have no degree. This job gives me an identity.

I'm finally somebody! I work for the government! This is big because I come from the wrong side of the tracks...but here there are rules about how people are treated, and I believe the environment is fair and equitable to everyone.

Wow, I've finally hit the jackpot! I rejoice. *This is like having a family! Here's my opportunity to work my way up! I work hard, follow the rules, and everyone likes me! My mom is wrong—I'm not going to end up on nerve pills!*

I set out to make something of myself. Promotions come easily to me. All I have to do is study and win the competition to move up. Always smart, I move ahead quickly. My bosses like me, I'm a top producer, and getting the job done is what matters.

A Normal Life

"What is it you really want?" my counselor asks me. Embarrassed and ashamed because I don't know, I realize no one's ever asked me that question before. My self-help journey begins when I start to consider the impact of having grown up in an alcoholic home.

A friend tells me about this woman named Louise Hay. She gives me a copy of a cassette tape filled with affirmations, which I listen to daily. I read her book, *You Can Heal Your Life,* but can't understand at first how I alone have the power to change anything.

I begin to realize how I'd lived in constant fear, knowing I had to be on high alert so I could protect myself and others from dangerous situations and circumstances. Never did I feel I had the power to create or change my life.

I try the affirmations, and feel better when I practice them. Suddenly I find a new job. I discover a support group—others who know what it means to have grown up in an alcoholic home. Over time, I begin to see progress and intuit that I can learn how to break free of the constraints that hide my heart.

I learn how to heal my woundedness by taking responsibility for my part. I work at forgiving my parents and others who've harmed me. I choose to understand that they did the best they could at the time. I make a conscious decision to carve out a different life for myself, to live free of alcohol and pills. I want to live a normal life with stability! I love my corporate government job, and soon marry an amazing man, buy a house, and become a mom!

How I Show Up

Overwhelmed with a feeling of complete forgiveness, I whisper to

Mom that despite our differences, I forgive her and have always truly loved her. I tell her I've come to be by her side as she transitions. I want her to feel safe.

I describe the peace and love she'll find on the other side and how she no longer needs to live in fear. I explain how her trauma, suffering, and pain will be over soon. I share my belief that her life is complete and that the time has come for her to cross over safely.

I watch as the machines are turned off and the tubes gently removed. She takes her last peaceful breath on the day of her seventy-fourth birthday. I feel the peace too, as difficult as it is, knowing that she's surrounded by family who have come together to support her highest good through great love.

I gain a deeper understanding that I have a greater purpose in life; that how I show up in the world matters. I realize I've never been alone—rather I've always been truly divinely guided. The universe created me—with a unique design and a grand plan I may not understand but am destined to carry out—a precious child!

ABOUT THE AUTHOR: As a natural leader and author, Brenda founded Heart Centered Solutions to create a safe space for personal development through mind, body and spirit. As a Licensed and Certified Heal Your Life® Teacher and Life Coach she teaches transformational techniques based on the philosophy of Louise Hay. During her thirty year career in the corporate arena, Brenda felt a calling to do something that really mattered. Her experience and training well equipped her for success in her second career providing opportunities for individuals to step into their best life!

Brenda Fedorchuk
Heart Centered Solutions
www.HeartCenteredSolutions.ca
Brenda@HeartCenteredSolutions.ca
306-550-3948

No More Lies

Carole Cassell

I lie in the fetal position on the floor of my closet, crying as Cruel-Ella wages a painful war within. Cruel-Ella is the name I give to the voice in my head that constantly berates me.

Relentless in her torture, usually I manage to drown her out. But tonight—tonight is different! Tonight is especially painful because deep down there is truth in her words. It *is* time for me to stop blaming my father, my childhood, my ex-husbands—all five of them...it *is* time to look deeper and take greater responsibility for my life.

However, right now the pain of my current situation is too great. Roger has lied to me for the millionth time and I can't take it anymore! I don't know how to go on.

Why doesn't he respect me, respect our marriage? How can this be happening again? Another man that doesn't value me! Why can't he see how much I love him?

These questions race through my mind, which is unable to hold a single thought for long. The idea of another marriage ending is more than I can bear.

My chest tight, I feel as if my heart is actually breaking. My face stings from the tears that stream down my cheeks. I pull my legs tightly into my chest and drift away. I just want to disappear...

"Babe, where are you"? Roger's voice startles me back to reality. His footsteps signal his approach. "Oh baby, what are you doing in there?"

His voice, so loving and filled with concern, is that of the man who lies to me regularly, who reaches into my chest and twists my heart like he's wringing out a wet rag. Now he's here to rescue me...from myself.

"Let me help you up honey, you need to come out of there."

He's right, I know he is. *What am I doing in here? I'm a forty-five year old woman lying in a ball on the floor of her closet!*

"I just hurt so badly," I whimper.

"I know" he says. "I'm sorry..."

He's sorry. Again. How many times have I heard that? His words infuriate me. Instantly I'm filled with rage.

"You're sorry? *Sorry?* I'll show you sorry!" My voice is harsh, deep, angry. "I hate you!" I scream and, as my rage turns to violence, I slap him across the face as hard as I can. "Leave me alone!"

He approaches me again.

"Leave me alone!" I sob as I kick at him.

Finally he leaves the room, but not for long. He never leaves me alone for long. His guilt won't let him.

The Unworthy

"You're a worthless piece of shit!" my father bellows, his six-foot frame towering over my skinny little body, his eyes filled with anger and hate. "You'll never amount to anything!" he adds, the stench of stale cigarettes on his breath.

My heart beats so fast I struggle to catch my breath, and my body trembles with fear. I fight to hold back the tears but they push their way through.

"Dry it up Carole—there's nothing to cry about!"

Scared and confused, I cower in fear, waiting for him to walk away so I can run to my room—my sanctuary—and seek refuge in my closet. He never bothers me in there. I'm safe in my closet.

As he leaves the room he turns and yells "that's right, go hide in your room, we don't want you out here anyway!" We've done this dance before.

"Don't listen to him honey," my mother reassures me once he's safely out of earshot. "You're a good girl and you can do whatever you set your mind to." Her words are of little consolation.

This is one scene of many in our obscene family play of pain, worthlessness, and inadequacy. Daddy's the star, the *Perfect One* and we're his supporting cast, *The Unworthy*. Sometimes I audition for other parts such as *The Helper, The Scholar, The Superstar*—whatever I think may win his favor, but alas, the only role he ever casts me in is *The Unworthy*.

I spend a sad number of years seeking Daddy's approval by becoming the best in everything I can.

"Look, Daddy, look!" I say with pride, kneeling before him as he sits on his throne, his sacred recliner. "I made the honor roll again!"

Time after time it isn't enough. Whether it's honor roll, captain of the cheerleading squad, first chair in band, medaling in track—it doesn't really matter, it will *never* be enough. It's clear I'll never win his love, approval, and validation.

The Whisper Of Hope

My sister, brother, and I lie in the back of the family station wagon late one night during one of our family vacations. Everyone's asleep except Daddy, who's driving, and me.

The click of his lighter, followed by the smell of his freshly lit cigarette excites my senses. I watch in a daze as the lights of the city flash by. Country music fills the air. The weight of the blanket provides comfort. I am, for the moment, peaceful.

I search my soul to try and understand why I'm such a bad person. I glance over at my sister and brother sleeping peacefully and wonder if they are going to be bad people too. Is our father right? Are none of us ever going to amount to anything?

For a moment I let my thoughts run wild, and a smile crosses my face as I see myself happy, successful, and loved—possibilities of what I can become. Suddenly I'm shocked out of my vision by a whisper in the dark:

*You are enough, you are capable of anything you desire, you are loved...*my mind races to make sense of this voice. Where did it come from? Is it God? Somehow, some way, in that moment, I believe that whisper...

Sixth Time's The Charm?

A few years after I hear the *whisper* I forget about it and begin to believe *his* words again—words that reaffirm I'll never be good enough, smart enough, or worthy enough. I leave home at sixteen with the man who will become my first husband. I'm hell-bent on creating a life of meaning, happiness, and love!

You know that saying "wherever you go, there you are?" It's so true. I bring my baggage of negative beliefs into every relationship. The phrase *you're a worthless piece of shit* takes up residence in my mind, reinforcing the basic premise that I am unlovable.

I jump from one marriage to another, eventually deeming either them or myself unworthy. I become a *serial bride*.

Often I attract men just like me. My first, second, and fourth husbands don't value themselves and are no more equipped to create a healthy marriage than I am. When I don't receive what I'm looking for, I move on.

In those moments where my light shines through, I attract men who *do* value me. In my third and fifth marriages I'm with two extremely good men, but I find ways to sabotage these relationships because of the deep belief I still hold that I'm unworthy of love.

My sixth husband Roger is a mix of them all. An incredibly loving man, filled with his own demons of worthlessness, doubt, and negativity, he carries as much baggage into the marriage as I do.

We struggle from the beginning. It's beyond tough, and many times I can't see how we'll make it. I like to think something more romantic is at play, but I believe the reality is that we're simply too stubborn to give up. I'm convinced a part of us needs the heartache; after all, we deserve it...

Deeming Myself Worthy

Six times, c'mon, something's got to give—it can't be all them and not me! It's not until this evening—spent on the floor of my closet—that I'm truly ready to surrender.

I'm open and ready to receive, I implore the universe, *what is it I need to do?* Finally, I let go of control and invite Spirit to lead the way. Thus begins my *true* personal healing journey.

Soon after, I'm given a vision of the next chapter of my life, and within months I'm guided to leave corporate America and start a wellness business. Along my new career path of assisting others on their journey to wellness, I'm introduced to the work of Louise Hay and Don Miguel Ruiz, both of whom accelerate my healing.

Their books become my nighttime companions, since Roger's away on business regularly. Although hungry for their teachings, the process is anything but easy.

"Bullshit!" I shout defiantly as I lob one of their books across the room. Did you know books can fly? Yeah, they can. My self-righteousness lasts only a moment before I find myself trudging over to pick it up and get back to the business of healing.

In their words I find a truth similar to what the *whisper* told me. Don Miguel's *The Four Agreements* teaches a way of living that brings enlightenment, peace, and understanding. Through Louise Hay's *You Can Heal Your Life* I find the lessons I need to heal and create the life I desire. I learn powerful tools of forgiveness and self-love, the tools I need to release myself from my mental prison.

I begin to realize everything that happens is of my own doing: *I* create my own reality and *I* choose each situation and every experience. Not always consciously, but through the beliefs I hold from the past. I learn to honor my journey and to better understand the choices I've made.

Six husbands and a lot of hard work later, I've finally stopped looking outside myself for validation. I know now that only I can determine my self-worth, and that inside me is a well of unlimited love, for myself as well as for others. I needn't look any further than my own heart!

I've since turned my anger and resentments into gratitude. Grateful to my father, mother, and five ex-husbands for the valuable, life-changing experiences we shared. I am especially grateful to my incredible husband Roger, who stood by me when I wasn't so loveable, and has owned the moments when he wasn't so loveable either. His support, both emotionally and financially, allows me to pursue my mission of assisting others as they heal their lives.

Our commitment to each other's growth and to our marriage has resulted in the life we dreamed of when we said "I do." As I stopped lying to myself about my own sense of self-worth, *he* stopped lying to me too, and the depth of love, openness, and support we offer each other is beyond my wildest dreams.

Finally, I can say without hesitation that I absolutely love myself *and* my life! No more lies about me being a worthless piece of shit...because...*I am worthy!*

ABOUT THE AUTHOR: What started as a personal healing journey became a passion that led to a new career when, in 2010, after 27 years in Corporate America, Carole resigned her position as Controller and began her wellness business. A Licensed Heal Your Life® Coach, Workshop Leader, Certified Health Coach and Licensed Massage Therapist, Carole uses her unique set of skills and practices to help her clients conquer chaos, create clarity and cultivate health by addressing the whole person: mind, body and spirit. Proud Mom to D.J. and Zach, and wife to Roger, Carole treasures her family and enjoys every second in their presence!

Carole Cassell
www.carolecassell.com
269-944-7305

Love Is The Strongest Force

Julie Jones Hamilton

"Mom, I'm so scared," I whimper to my mother between tears in the hallway of her lovely home in the California desert. "I've never been so filled with fear! I feel paralyzed—like I may not live through this—I don't know what choice to make!"

"Julie, I support you in whatever decision you make," she answers, holding me tight. "If you want to come and live with me, you can. If you want to stay in Lexington, that's fine too. However, you must make a choice—being in limbo is just too painful."

"But I don't know what to do with my life now!"

"Make the choice that gives you life," Mom answers softly in her comforting way.

In Los Angeles for a *Miracle Mastery* seminar, seeking to discover a new way to live, I've left behind Jimmy, my vital, handsome, successful entrepreneur husband of twenty years. Worth millions, he's systematically disassembled his entire fortune in a patent infringement lawsuit with Google, one of the largest software giants on the planet.

I'd left him asleep in our darkened bedroom in what appeared to be a deepening depression. The ruling against him proved such a shock that it left him bedridden in disbelief—and me on the front lines of the battlefield to sort through the wreckage.

Until recently my life as a wife, mother, and community volunteer and fundraiser was all I ever wanted. I love it! I love being married to Jimmy. I love being a former president of my favorite non-profit agency, a member of the board of trustees at my son's private school, the social life, jet-setting vacations, our mansion in Lexington, Kentucky, and our second home on the beach in south Florida.

I love being invited to all the parties, able to buy anything I want and attend sixteen straight Kentucky Derby Horse Races on

Millionaire Row.

Then, suddenly, in one swift verdict, life as I know it evaporates. Literally overnight, like watching the dew melt on the blades of grass under the sun, all I've known for twenty years disappears before my eyes in slow motion. The money gone, the invitations stop, and the bills pile up. Our resources exhausted, we file for bankruptcy, and foreclosure on our home is obvious.

And all the while, my commander in chief, my faithful leader and staunchest supporter slips deeper into the black abyss of depression. In survivor mode, I'm left to rear our teenage son Gunnar, make complicated business decisions, and address employees. I'm to sell whatever assets we have in order to keep a roof over our heads and food on the table.

With no college education, no business training, no relationships with bankers or business people, I soldier on not really knowing what to do or if and when Jimmy will reemerge to rescue me. I sell everything of value—jewelry, furniture, clothes, books, and art. I take baby steps rattled with fear, anxiety, public embarrassment, and lots of uncontrollable sobbing.

Part of me wants to be the one in bed. Each day I grow more weary and broken. I want to let this life wash over me and be done. The continued pressure of what to do next goes beyond putting out fires. It's like I'm living inside the blue heat of a blazing fire.

"Ends Are Not Bad Things, They Just Mean That Something Else Is About To Begin." ~ C. Joybell C.

I enter adulthood when I leave my father's home and move in with the first man who ever says he loves me. I don't ask what I can bring to the marriage, I think only of what I can get out of it.

I'm twenty years old and John's a successful restaurant owner able to provide me the luxury of being a stay at home mom when our two little girls come along. Ten years into our marriage, however, I realize that the foundation of most marriages is mutual commitment based on love.

Truth be told, I'm not deeply in love with John and realize I'm living a lie. Soon I'm unable to look at myself in the mirror until I tell him the truth. Unfortunately, John doesn't take kindly to my newfound awareness, and a bitter and messy divorce ensues.

Young, happy, and free, I ask my single mother to move in with me to help care for the girls while I work. Times are tough but bittersweet as Mom and I do our best to support each other. One weekend, while my daughters visit their father, I suggest we go out for a bite to eat.

"Who knows, maybe we'll meet someone," I say.

After a lovely meal we hear the rapid strumming of an exotic flamingo guitar float out from the lounge as we're exiting the restaurant. My mother grabs my elbow and directs me back into the lounge.

"See that tall man over there—the tallest one on the dance floor?" she asks as she sways to the music. I don't see anyone tall, only a lot of people and a smoky lounge. Mom finds a table, we sit down, and she motions to a table of men where "Mr. Tall" is sitting. She points to me and waves him over.

Mortified, I look up to see Mr. Tall. He asks me to dance. I hide my embarrassment with a big smile.

"My name is Jimmy Hamilton from Lexington, Kentucky," he says on the dance floor. "I've been married and divorced twice, have five grown children, and I'm available. Are you?"

"Yes," I stutter, surprised.

"I've been praying to the 'Big Man' and for two years I've looked for someone, and I believe you may be her."

We then begin a long distance whirlwind courtship. After a year he moves twenty-seven boxes, my daughters, and me to Lexington, Kentucky, where we wed. Extremely generous, he provides the girls with the best education and we go on thrilling vacations.

He's exciting, owns several companies, and supports us in the lap of luxury. We're blessed beyond words! He even offers a home for my mother, who moves to Kentucky to be near us.

To top it off, we conceive a son. When Gunnar turns five, Mom moves back to the warmer climate of California where she falls in love and begins a long-term relationship.

"Sometimes Things Fall Apart So That Better Things Fall Together." ~ Unknown

Now I find myself in the arms of my mother, filled with fear about making my decision: do I stay in Kentucky with Jimmy, who *may* revert to the vibrant, successful man I married, or do I pick up the pieces and start my life over in California near my mother?

Still vibrant and young, what if I can meet someone who'll take care of me? I will have security. Isn't that the root of my fear—worry about being alone, without a husband or financial support?

I retreat into one of my mother's lovely guest rooms. During the next three days of pain, prayer, and meditation—without self-pity or blame—I float above my body and look down at myself. I begin to awaken to a deeper, invisible part of me. I realize I'm so much more than simply a body and a personality.

When was the last time I believed in myself—really believed in my capacity to generate love? I wonder. *Aren't I always looking for others to fill that need inside of me?*

It's then I begin to notice something more as the basis of my drama: the pattern of choices I've made in my life. The times I've escaped from uncomfortable situations into an easier, softer way out. I use this escape route to avoid facing my feelings, pain, and belief in myself.

I use people, places, and things to keep the focus off of *me*. Dependent upon others and what they say and do for my own happiness, I know deep down inside the decision I'm about to make will shift the trajectory of my life.

I now understand that every choice I've made up until now—consciously or subconsciously—has brought me to this pivotal moment—for the first time I see *I'm* the cause of all the effects in my life!

Am I willing to stand on the foundation of a love greater than myself, a pure, positive love that penetrates, permeates, and fills the inner spaces of the universe? The kind of indwelling love, a higher order of love that surpasses all human conditions and suffering, the love I've read about in stories throughout history?

This thread of love connects everything and everyone. I realize I'm in this life to experience, laugh and grow, share and give, care and love! I understand how I've misplaced my dependency on things outside myself, and see clearly how disconnected from inner source, strength, and self-love I am.

"What's the opposite of fear?" I ask myself in this moment.

Faith! I hear a voice say.

"What do I place my faith on?"

On pure love, on self–love, for love is the strongest force in the universe!

I've heard the longest human journey is the eighteen inches from our head to our heart.

Return To A Place Of Love

Suddenly, I know I will be all right! Still afraid, nevertheless I realize I'm willing to bet on love, regardless of what it looks like, and immediately I feel expansive!

I make my decision: I choose to love my marriage, my situation, and my life, no matter what! Didn't my husband place his faith on a prayer when we first met? Hadn't we shared years of plenitude and happiness as a result? Now I'm willing to walk through whatever conditions I experience because I know there's something greater than myself supporting me.

I can see where I've allowed prestige, societal pressure, and my own ego get in the way. I acknowledge—even though I honor the more sincere and noble actions I took—that I used a lot of my wealth, connections, and opportunities for selfish motives to satisfy my own ego.

I return home and begin to see Jimmy differently. I hold him in the eyes of love and glorify in his perfection. Slowly, he begins to reemerge. With therapy and a strong men's support group, the man I thought I lost comes back, more endearing and loving than ever!

In the end, our experience allows us a greater understanding of love, and teaches us to build our muscles in faith and to trust in a benevolent and abundant universe that always supports our greater good.

Now Jimmy utilizes his gifts and talents to build a new life and company, and I use each moment to align in profound gratitude. Together, we understand that indeed *love is the strongest force...*

ABOUT THE AUTHOR: The founder of *The Empowerment Foundation Group, LLC,* and *Julie Jones Hamilton International Consulting,* Julie consults professionals, groups, churches, and entrepreneurs to create results, realize dreams, and accelerate success in building a blueprint for a life they love. As co-founder of *The Four Dames,* she offers self-development interactive workshops, courses, and programs. The Four Dames are authors of the soon-to-be-published book *The 12 Absolute Laws of Creating Wealth, Starting Today!* Julie has served thousands of women reclaim inner-power from substance dependency as former president and board member for 24 years, at the renowned long-term treatment agency, *The Chrysalis House,* in Lexington KY.

Julie Jones Hamilton
www.juliejoneshamilton.com
julie@juliejoneshamilton.com
859-229-5939

PART THREE

Conscious
Spirituality

"The only place the mind will ever find peace
is inside the silence of the heart.
That's where you need to go."
~ Elizabeth Gilbert

Meant For Something Better

Dixie Rivera

My grandmother is the only mother I know until I'm six years old. My mother's choice to leave me with her when I'm nine months old, while she settles into a new area and a new life, undoubtedly seems to her like a good idea at the time.

However, the house my grandmother lives in is poorly built and partially under construction. Mostly exposed to the outside, only a small portion of the house is enclosed.

In addition, my grandmother's house has become the neighborhood shelter for every stray dog and cat around. She feeds at least forty dogs and cats daily and manages to take care of me, but it doesn't take long to realize I've been placed in a chaotic and unsanitary situation.

My memory of my grandmother during this time is not a loving one. A very abrasive woman with little patience, no tolerance, and a quick hand, she's also a hoarder. Although I recall having fun with the neighborhood kids and visiting other relatives sometimes, most of my good memories are overshadowed by recollections of dangerously close calls with some of the animals. I watch some die of illness or from attacks by other animals, including those to which I've grown close.

I recall my mother visiting me once at my grandmother's house and wonder if it means she's coming to take me home. She's with a gentleman to whom I feel no connection. It turns out to be a brief visit, and I don't see her again for some time. A tough situation, it's a lot for me to deal with as a child, and I hope and pray that my mom will come get me.

Finally that day comes. I remember clearly my aunt arriving in a taxi. My grandmother dresses me as if we're going somewhere, but she's not dressed to leave the house. My aunt comes in and they converse briefly. I feel a lot of sadness from them both.

Confused, I don't understand what's happening. I watch the taxi driver load suitcases into the trunk of the car. My aunt leads me into the back of the taxi. Still I don't realize I'm leaving until I turn around and see my grandmother standing outside watching us drive away.

Suddenly, it hits me like a freight train—she's taking me away! I'm leaving the only home I know, the only mother I know! I begin to cry and look back at my grandmother until I can no longer see her. I thought that this is what I wanted, but the reality turns out to be heartbreaking...

"Already I'm So Lonesome I Could Die..." ~ Joni Mitchell, *Leaving On A Jet Plane*

The taxi arrives at my new home. I'm tired and confused. Although only six, I'm angry with my aunt for "taking" me but then realize she's "taking" me to my mother. I feel so disconnected, like everyone around me knows what's going on except me. They keep talking about me like I'm not here. Finally, I have no choice but to start settling in.

I like that I have my own room, a nice house, and a fenced-in yard. I begin to appreciate being with my mother although she feels like a stranger.

Now I'll finally have a safe and stable home, I think, *and can live a normal life!* I don't have a clear idea exactly what that will be, but even at this young age I know it isn't the life I've been living.

Unfortunately, my joy is short lived. The man who accompanied my mother during her visit to my grandmother's house years before—the one with whom I felt no connection—lives with my mother. Shortly after I arrive, he starts molesting me sexually. I go from living with an abusive hoarder to being exposed to sexual, physical, and emotional abuse.

Prior to this time my life isn't great, but I'm a still child and have some semblance of internal joy. Expressive, I like to have fun and wish for the same things most kids do. This move changes me, and I become isolated, introverted, very alone, and think: *no one can understand what I'm going through!*

The sexual abuse continues. Horribly afraid to say anything to anyone, *who's going to believe me?* I worry. I get the courage to try to talk to my mother when I'm nine. Invited to a wedding, she's getting dressed to go and I beg her to take me with her.

I know once she leaves, I'll be alone with *him.* I know he'll take advantage of this and have his way with me. Sometimes he abuses me when my mother is home, and I dread the idea of her going to this wedding without me because it's always worse when she's away.

I don't want to be left alone with him! I seize on an opportune time to tell my mother when he walks away briefly. Desperate because I know she'll be away for hours, I cry and beg her not to leave me, but she dismisses me and sweeps it under the rug, just like everything else.

That night I suffer the beating of my life. He'd heard what I said to my mother and makes sure I know that. He's drinking, as usual, and so angry that I don't think I'll make it through the night.

After this experience, I know my mother's not going to be there for me the way I need her to be. I can't talk to her because she simply looks the other way and pretends nothing is going on. This almost kills me.

Time To Be Happy

The years of abuse and loneliness become so bad I want to take my own life, and at fifteen I decide to end my pain for good—to end it all. I don't feel worthy to continue. By this time, I've experienced sexual abuse by other adult men, including the babysitter's brother, another relative, and a neighbor's father on a playdate.

Twice I plan to end it all. Somehow, though, I decide not to go through with it. Although I have such a difficult relationship with my mother, I consider what this would do to her—*and* I don't want to leave her alone. I guess in some way I understand she's a victim also.

Something deep inside keeps me alive. Even though it's difficult, I believe I'm meant for something better. *There's a reason I need to be alive,* I think.

Shortly afterward, something inside clicks, and I realize *no one's going to come to my rescue—I'm the only one who can change this situation. I can't allow this to define the rest of my life!* Angry and disgusted, I decide to confront him and put a stop to the abuse.

It takes every ounce of courage to fight back, but I do! Though I've been led to believe otherwise, I suspect he's not really my biological father—a fact I later confirm. I tell him he's under-estimated me, and encourage him to give it a shot if he doesn't think this is the case. I make it clear that if he ever touches me again, I'll tell the world, starting with the police.

For years he's told me how he grew up and survived on the

streets after losing his father in childhood.

"If your life was so horrible, why would you recreate it for another child?" I ask him. "Do you not see that I'm also trying to survive? Don't you understand *you've* created this world I live in?" *I'm not my mother,* I think, *I'm going to react and now that I'm older I know I have other options, even if that means running away.*

Terrified, I wonder what will happen now—the next few minutes, hours, days? *Will he try to keep me quiet? What now?*

The days pass and there's a strange quiet in the house. I've set myself physically free from his abuse, but how to become emotionally free? I decide I want a great life—and a family! I know the best thing I can do is not to repeat the vicious cycle that almost consumed me. It's time for me to be happy!

"Forgive Others, Not Because They Deserve Forgiveness But Because You Deserve Peace." ~ Jonathan Lockwood Huie

I make the decision to care more about myself. I realize I can live in fear or envision a wonderful future with a beautiful family.

After spending some time focusing on personal development, I find meditation extremely helpful. It allows me to feel a stronger spiritual connection and to seek the guidance I so desperately need. Drawn to the elements of earth, I feel most connected when near water.

A constant work in progress, my happiness doesn't come overnight. But I hang in there—onto the fire in my belly—the one that speaks to me and tells me I'm meant for greater things!

One day, after attending a spiritual development workshop, I begin to meditate while in the shower. I intuit it's time to start the process of forgiving myself.

I close my eyes and take myself back to when I'm a child. My mind drifts to my mother's house—I feel the warm air and see the colors of my surroundings. A small rancher, tan with brown trim, beautiful palm trees and hedges line the walkway.

My small swing set is on the side of the house, and there I am—a sweet, innocent little girl—wearing an outfit I truly hate as my mother photographs me with my "father." Significant because I recall really disliking the bell bottoms and green plaid jacket with matching tie, every time I see this picture it stirs up much resentment and pain.

I take little Dixie's face in my hands and let her know how much I love her. I tell her that none of what happened was her fault—that the situation was out of her control. I let her know how beautiful she is. I thank her for hanging in there and getting us through—it's her inner light that saved us!

I tell her I'm so proud of her, and that we're doing great things now because of her! I appreciate her with all my heart and tell her it's time to forgive herself.

This proves life-changing as the immense pain and heartache start to leave, released through my tears.

Epilogue

Married now with five amazing children, I realize the value of letting go. Forgiveness is a huge factor in being able to heal and move forward. Although I've still had struggles finding my identity, and hardships—a failed marriage and lots of self-sabotaging behavior—I've worked hard on self-improvement and now focus on surrounding myself with good people.

My continual search for a deeper sense of being and a higher spiritual connection teaches me to value myself, and reinforces the inner *knowing* that I'm meant for something better.

ABOUT THE AUTHOR: The proud owner and lead designer of *Interior Passions Kitchen & Bath,* Dixie Rivera knows the kitchen is the heart of any home and the bath is a homeowner's retreat. A true entrepreneur, Dixie puts the "passion" into *Interior Passions* and offers her clients the ideal combination of creativity, personal attention, knowledge, and contacts within the kitchen and bath industry to ensure stress-free, pleasant design experiences. Certified in decorative painting, design, interior decorating, and applied arts—and with a strong background in retail business—Dixie's dream to help others set the stage where beautiful memories are created happens every day!

Dixie Rivera
www.interiorpassions.com
drivera@interiorpassions.com
dixierivera@gmail.com
856-228-8989

Divine Intervention
Katherine Nuyens

I take my religion seriously—so much so, that by the eighth grade I insist on becoming a nun. Scared that God won't love me if I fail to please Him, I begin a life of perfectionism ruled by fear, and determine to be the best me at a young age.

A gentle sensitive soul, I trust—and act on—the voice within when it tells me to enroll at a convent school hundreds of miles away from home. I attend this school for two years, and my timing is synchronistic—I learn later that while away my older sister became pregnant and all hell broke out in our home.

After two years I fail to appreciate the structure of the school and return home, though I wonder: *was I protected from this challenging time—safely hundreds of miles away—because I listened to my heart?* At this time in my life I do not realize that everything is in divine order, and that there are no mistakes in the universe.

When The Student Is Ready, The Teacher Appears

My first teaching job arrives in 1970 and I'm a passionate teacher! When I receive a call the summer of 1982 informing me that I'm laid off, I'm devastated and angry. I yell at God for the unfairness of it—grade school teachers like me replaced by high school teachers with more seniority? These teachers don't want to teach grade school!

Intuition directs me to open the Bible and ask *why?* I do as directed, and land immediately on the passage from the Last Supper where Jesus explains: *You don't understand now what I am doing, but later you will understand.* I begin to realize that everything is in divine order and there really are no mistakes.

Losing my teaching position turns out to be one of my biggest life changes, and yes, one of my most significant synchronicities.

The timing turns out to be great in the scheme of things though, since my daughter Laurie is to start kindergarten in the fall. Laid off with my best friend, we have a ball experiencing many different activities.

The following year I'm hired to teach at a Catholic school where I have to learn a whole new philosophy of education called *The Workshop Way*, geared toward building confidence and self-esteem in children. During this training, I learn this concept for myself and realize it's time now for me to let go of my need for perfectionism.

My biggest gift during this period is meeting Sister Eileen Cordes, who teaches me about *A Course in Miracles,* channeling, and metaphysics. Being such a devout Catholic, it makes sense that these new understandings would have to be introduced to me by a nun or a priest. Unusual for a nun to think this much outside the box of Catholicism, Sister Eileen changes my life and I realize God has gifted her to me!

A Course in Miracles is a self-study curriculum that aims to assist individuals to achieve spiritual transformation and to "remove the blocks to the awareness of love's presence, which is your inheritance." It begins with: "Nothing real can be threatened. Nothing unreal exists. Herein lies the peace of God."

Not long after, I attend a gathering to hear a metaphysical speaker and meet Jane, with whom I connect easily. A few weeks later, when a metaphysical event is held in our area, I keep hearing that I should invite Jane. I hesitate, fearing she may not remember me, even though we'd exchanged telephone numbers. When the message repeats several times, I call Jane and we become great friends. She introduces me to a group of women who gather together for spiritual discussions and meditations. The timing of meeting Jane is another powerful synchronicity in my life. Our group participates in the first harmonic convergence of 1987.

The Voice Within

Back in the public school system now, and after teaching just short of twenty years, I realize that students need more than reading, writing, and arithmetic—they need counseling. I approach the superintendent and request he hire me as an elementary school counselor. He agrees and I pursue my M.A. in Counseling Psychology. I spend five years as an elementary school counselor, but feel burned out after only four because I'm too sensitive and can't turn off my emotions when I leave school.

At this time, I belong to another powerful group of four women who meet monthly to share spiritual understandings and experience healings. They notice my overwhelm, know I have only five more years (out of the necessary thirty) until retirement, and encourage me to leave. When my twenty-fifth year comes around, I fail to get excited. This is a first for me.

I meditate often before school, and one November morning I decide to request a *clear sign* if I need to leave the school. The very next day I receive in the mail a free sample of an angel tarot card that reads "Surrender." I can't deny the truth of that message, so with my husband's support, I purchase five years and buy myself early retirement in June 1998.

One blustery Saturday in January, as I'm driving to meet a friend for breakfast, my head is spinning with confusion and fear about my decision to retire early. I've taught my whole adult life, and frankly, I like the paycheck! Part of me is tuned into my fear of the future, while one ear is listening to Wayne Dyer on cassette.

"Your thoughts create your reality," is the last thing I hear him say as I slide into the car ahead of me! Though the car is undamaged, I'm angry with myself. I know with certainty my negativity and low vibrational level caused my accident.

You feel enough guilt, no need for anymore, I hear. I get the lesson—I have to learn to mind my mind!

Later, I find myself attending a class in self mastery, and when asked the qualities of my ideal job, I write "visionary," and wonder *where did that come from?* I write also that I want my work to be my play with flexible hours, to be self-enhancing, and to bring me joy and abundance. I send my list out to the universe and wait.

A response comes back to me a couple of months later when I read a newspaper article about an artist who no longer feels creative. After receiving hypnosis, her creativity resumes and she's once again painting beautiful art. I decide to try hypnosis in case I have any creative blocks.

After the session, the hypnotist invites me to learn hypnosis through her upcoming class. Goosebumps up and down my spine tell me it's a big *yes!* Everyone picks a tarot card during our first class, and she announces that this is how we'll use hypnosis. Initially embarrassed to admit that I've drawn *the Fool* card, I learn that this card means my work will be my play, and that the universe will support me. Synchronicities are now even more abundantly clear in my life!

Independence

My husband Tom, laid off after 9/11, adamantly declares that he won't relocate to find another job. I've already started my new work and realize there's a whole world out there for us to investigate. "I might have to fly alone!" I announce to him, filled with judgment and frustration. Honestly, I'm taken aback at myself, as I have no idea from where this thought derives.

I meet Edward while attending a hypnosis convention. When spirit asks me to request a testimonial for a workbook I've just completed, called *Invitation to Greatness*, I hear the message, listen, and act, but it's humbling. Yet he says he's honored and we become friends. We meet again two years later, but this time it feels more like a soul connection. I hear clearly that it's time to leave my husband of thirty-three years.

At this point in my life, I've learned to trust my messages, and know that all of my divine interventions have been for my highest good—but this is over the top! Shocked and dismayed, I think *this can't be true! Everyone knows our great love for one another. This makes no sense!*

I absolutely love Tom, and Edward is fully aware of our wonderful relationship. Yet, when Edward and I are together at the conference everyone notices we are connected.

I request not just one clear sign, but *three*. I receive even more! Through a medium, my mom comes through and congratulates me on my courage to leave Tom. She acknowledges that it's for my personal spiritual growth. She tells me that Tom's a good man and will find another to love.

Next Tom's father comes through and tells me: "If I was on your side of the veil, I wouldn't understand why you have to leave Tom, but I'm on the other side and see the whole picture." I wish I'd asked him more about the whole picture!

I move to New Jersey in 2003 to be with Edward, and together we open a hypnosis center. I cry many nights for the security of Tom and can't see what the universe has in mind. My daughter, now on her own, fails to understand and withdraws from me. Defeated, I don't know *why or how*, but choose to continue trusting my signs from spirit.

This experience proves to be my greatest life challenge, and my best teacher. I begin to see the synchronicities: later I hear *we had to introduce you to Edward to pull you away from Tom because you need to be a more independent female—you came into this life to be independent.* Another time, while driving over a bridge to visit a friend, spirit even yells at me *"you don't need a man!"*

Eventually I come to believe my real lesson is learning to move into my own power, and I leave the center and the relationship. I create my own business and add a number of new healing modalities besides hypnosis to my practice. My daughter and I resume our close relationship, and Tom and I never fully disconnect; our past is too powerful.

Tom is very happy now and married to my college roommate, which helps release my guilt. I love being alone, independent, coming home and having quiet, even though I have a new man in my life—one with whom I understand I have a soul contract to be together. The angels assure me I've learned well.

I understand synchronicity as a "God involved" event, and realize now that God is *unconditional love, all that is,* and not a being who judges our every action. As I look back on my life and know that there were no mistakes, I am in awe and grateful that so many significant events were guided by the voice within and by divine intervention.

ABOUT THE AUTHOR: Katherine Nuyens has a Master's in Counseling Psychology and is certified in Hypnosis with the National Guild. For twenty five years Katherine served as an elementary teacher and school counselor in Michigan Public Schools. After teaching, Katherine was guided to learn a number of healing modalities and is passionate about this present work. Her newest certification is *The Emotion Code/Body Code,* finding and releasing imbalances in the body. Because everything is energy, her practice is not limited locally. Katherine has served clients all over the U.S. You can visit Katherine at empoweringchangeinyou.com. She offers free consults.

Katherine Nuyens
Empowering Change, LLC
Marlton, NJ
www.empoweringchangeinyou.com
856-780-5302

Fall Into Grace

Gina Medvedz

I pick up my cell phone to dial Tara's number just as the screen lights up with an incoming call bearing her name.

"I was just about to call you!" I laugh in amazement into the phone. "I need Lori's number!"

I think back to a time more than a year ago when my dear friend Tara invites me to a ladies lunch at her home with a few mutual friends. Also present is a woman named Lori who reads the akashic records. Although I have no idea what these are, I'm always up for a new experience and decide to have a reading.

"The askashic records are an ethereal library of every soul's journey up to and including your present lifetime," Lori explains. After reading a short prayer to open my records, she asks, "what would you like to know?"

I stare at her blankly.

"I'm not a psychic," she explains. "Rather, I communicate with your teachers and guides who are here with me to help you with any of your current struggles."

The only thing I can think to ask about is my business. A nutritional consultant—with a bachelor's degree in education and a master's in holistic nutrition—I educate people about optimal health through nutrition, and work primarily with those recovering from chronic disease.

Although I'm passionate about my career, business is slow. While my clients *do* experience success, a gnawing feeling deep inside tells me something is missing. I intuit that I should be doing more for them, and that in addition to nutritional counseling they need to heal from the root problems causing them to misuse food and mistreat their bodies. I fear I've chosen the wrong field of work not once, but twice, and wonder if I'm supposed to be doing some type of ministry work instead.

My reading is incredibly enlightening and leaves me tremendously uplifted and motivated. Lori tells me I'm an incredible healer, and that powerful, healing archangels surround me, waiting for me to assist them in God's work here on Earth, but that I'm standing in my own way.

Can this be true? I wonder. Overwhelmed by the responsibility this information implies, I nevertheless can't seem to shake my fears. I *know* I'm standing in my own way, and Lori's message ignites a spark deep inside and fills me with the knowledge that I can no longer delay. Armed with the names of the archangels Raphael and Haniel, I begin to pray to them for courage and healing.

Shortly afterward, I decide to invite Lori over to my home to read for my family and friends, but that's when life gets in the way...

Playing Small

My whole life I feel such pressure to succeed. The only person in my family to attend college, I know I am expected to accomplish something impressive and I carry this burden of expectation into my professional life. Deep inside something keeps nudging me, telling me I'm destined for something greater.

My husband Paul and I have the perfect relationship, healthy children, and every material item we want and yet somehow something's missing. I push the feeling away by focusing my attention on the problems and needs of others. A psychologist for my friends, and the type of person who says yes to even the craziest of requests, I run myself ragged volunteering wherever I can.

People tell me my knowledge is impressive, and while I know there's no shortage of potential clients with chronic disease who need me, I'm paralyzed. *I should be teaching workshops,* I think, but then become incapable of finding a place to hold them. An irrational fear of using the telephone and the thought of co-partnering to promote my business leave me shaking. Ironically, when doing business as the vice-president of my church or the president of my sorority alumnae group, I can call anyone.

It seems my fear is based strictly upon low self-worth and the underestimation of the value of my services. The thought of failing scares me so that I make sure success doesn't happen by claiming to be bad at marketing and too busy to network. If nobody knows who I am or what I do professionally, then I can continue in my role as a fabulous mother and wife.

It's not fair that I have so many fears! I'm a better speaker and more educated than many of my peers, and yet somehow they're in the spotlight as I watch *their* videos and read *their* books. I attend seminars and attempt to learn successful business skills, though that's not what I need—I need a miracle that will cleanse me of my fears and lack of self-love.

I grow bitter and find myself wondering why everyone else seems to make strides in their lives while I'm stuck in neutral.

Shock & Awe

Tragedy strikes when my family—Paul, our two teenage children, and I—survive a head-on car collision. The first time anything like this has ever happened, we lose our car but amazingly the four of us walk out of the crumpled vehicle in one piece.

Four months later the four of us stand together again—this time in our neighbor's driveway—and look on in horror as flames crawl across our garage and threaten to devour our home. Our garage is destroyed, and the smoke damage is so severe that the entire house needs to be gutted and rebuilt on the inside.

Together we bounce from a hotel—where initially we have nothing but two outfits each—to a rented townhome. Finally, we encamp with my sister and her family for the last two months of our painstakingly long nine-month house renovation.

Throughout the ordeal, although our nerves are raw, somehow we know intrinsically that we need to laugh a lot to keep up with our daily routines. Minimal possessions remain, and this actually turns out to be very freeing for us all. I realize I don't need *things*—it's not the possessions in life that matter, it's the people and the love. I'm blessed and thankful that I'm able now to focus one-hundred percent on family and myself. Self-care is something I need to catch up on...

"Love Is The Crowning Grace Of Humanity..." ~ Francesco Petrarch

"I just signed up for a class to become certified to read the akashic records, and thought you might like to join me," Tara says, revealing the reason for her call.

"Yes!" I answer immediately. Since my return home, I am determined to have Lori read my akashic records again. I want to experience the love I felt previously and receive further guidance about my life. Changed for the better by the fire, I'm even more aware now that my clients have spiritual work to do if they want to heal completely. I hope Lori can help me—I have no idea how to incorporate such a mission into my nutrition practice.

We travel to New Jersey from our homes in Pennsylvania and nervous anticipation fills my stomach with butterflies. *What if I can't do this?* It never occurred to me I might not be successful in this endeavor. I have no psychic or medium skills and begin to worry excessively.

We spend time the first night getting acquainted with sixteen other women there for the weekend. One is a psychic, but everyone else is not, and I am comfortable knowing that I'm not alone in my inexperience. The next morning we learn about the history of the records, how they can clear phobias and resentments, and sometimes help explain and repair physical illness. Lori guides us through an exercise that teaches us to discern between information received through the records and that which we intuit.

The results surprise me—based on my own intuition, I believe my life's purpose is to teach others how to eat for optimal health. However, when we open our records as a group and I ask them my life purpose, it turns out it has nothing to do with nutrition at all!

Your life purpose is to teach self-love and to extend grace, I'm shocked to see the words I write in my notebook. *Grace? What does that mean?* I wonder. I *never* use the word *grace*—to me it's something so intangible!

You are to recognize the good in others and bring it to their awareness, I hear next as clearly as if my guides are right here with me. This resonates so deeply that I feel honored and overwhelmed to be entrusted with such noble work.

There's one problem, though. I don't really love myself. I can see so clearly what's wonderful about everyone else, but in my own eyes I'm not smart, educated, certified, or—most importantly of all—worthy enough.

"How can I teach self-love when I don't love myself?" I ask. In that moment I experience a deep knowing that it won't be that way anymore. As if bathing in a sea of love, all of my worries and fears suddenly dissolve and wash away. I hear Lori's voice faintly in the background guiding the exercise but I'm too blissfully wrapped in the infinite love of the universe to pay her any attention.

Realization races through my mind while tears stream down my cheeks. *I am amazing! I am perfect! I am not broken! I don't need to be fixed! I'm the exact version of myself that I need to be and the universe is waiting for me to step into my light and shine. I am the only thing that has ever stopped my progress. The universe holds me in love and glory, and longs for my happiness!*

Epilogue

I emerge from this experience a changed woman. I *know* I'm the one who's been keeping myself small, so I release my fear and decide to view myself the way I am seen in the eyes of God.

Each day I open my records and ask *what do I need to do today?* Some days the answer is simple and I have to call my mother, or vacuum. Others, the answers are challenging and test my newfound bravado. Always, though, these answers move me forward and improve my life.

Encouraged to write a novel, lead workshops, and teach at the local community college, I've also been led to create my *Guided Nutrition* program—a nutrition consultation inside the akashic records of a client—and taken it to mind, body, and spirit fairs throughout the country.

Reading the akashic records has taught me that I'm not alone. Our masters, teachers, loved ones, angels, and God are all here to provide divine guidance. Once I align myself with that guidance by asking, listening, and taking action, my fears and struggles melt away and simply fall into grace.

ABOUT THE AUTHOR: Rev. Gina Medvedz is a Certified Akashic Records reader, spiritual healer and Certified Nutritional Consultant with an M.S. in Holistic Nutrition. Ordained in the Order of Melchizedek, she uses divine guidance to clear the fear and self-doubt that prevents her clients from living an inspired life. Her passion lies in reconnecting people with their spirit guides and teaching them to bring all areas of their lives into alignment with their soul's purpose. Gina speaks globally about transformation and her message of healing through self-love. She is currently publishing her first novel, Sarah Starts Living, to be released in January 2015.

Rev. Gina Medvedz, MS, CNC
Wellness Transformations
www.wellnesstransformations.com
gina@wellnesstransformations.com

Our Life Tells Our Birth Story: How Babies Helped Me Heal

Eliza Parker

Wise Baby

"I'm ready now, you can push," I tell baby Bennett, situated in my lap, his feet on my belly. He's been wailing for ten minutes even though he's neither hungry nor sleepy.

He gears up with a few small pushes. His searching feet look for that just right spot where he'll have the most power, feeling through it with an intense internal wisdom.

His head searches too. How does he know what he's looking for? His feet keep trying, but he won't launch himself until he can get it just right. A buzzing sensation arises somewhere in the depths of my gut. I know where this sensation is headed so I look around for a box of tissues.

Suddenly, he finds it! The push of his all-knowing feet shoots like an arrow through his spine, and he moves head-ward away from me. His body travels in a slight arch backward, spiraling to his left. I'm not moving him, but following, making it possible for him to fly through space.

This amazing little guy is replaying his birth! Well, it seems like flying through space now. When he first did this, he traversed the brilliant tunnel of his mother's pelvic bones—shaped with two oblong openings perpendicular to each other to allow the spiral-like passing through of his head, then his shoulders.

I ride with him, one hand behind his head and one on his torso so I can flip my hands over to support him when he spirals. I marvel at the efficiency of his glide, like a train zooming in its track.

Huh, what would it have been like, I wonder, *to push and find myself in a mysterious tunnel, being spiraled by unseen walls, squeezing through a tight space, compression against my face, exiting...into...*

Oops! Back to task. This baby, gliding so expertly a split second ago, has suddenly stopped. Lying there on his tummy with his face to the right, but his legs flailing, he's showing me his birth story. More than showing me, he's still trying to work it out for himself at three months old.

It's as if he's saying to me "there's just something about this spot! I got stuck here, and I just don't know what happened! My body says to keep moving, but I can't, and I'm so frustrated! I won't feel resolved until I figure this out!"

We've done this three times now, each time stopping in the same place. He cries even harder. I'm feeling rather emotional myself now.

"Do you feel stuck?" I ask as I lie down beside him. He cries in response. Instead of picking him up and starting over like the two times before, I wonder if he can figure it out if we simply stay here together. After all, look at the internal brilliance that got him this far.

"Bennett, I hear you. Yeah, I see! What do you need?" I wait. "What if I give you something to push against while you're on your tummy?" I place my flat palms against his feet. He jabs. And wriggles.

"Wow, you're really working at this," I mumble to myself. The jabbing escalates into pushes that inch through his spine. Eventually he's able to push his whole body forward. He lifts his head, looks around—and stops crying.

Just like that. Calm, peaceful, and back to the day's play.

Meanwhile, I have a river growing inside of me looking for an exit.

"Um...I'll be right back!" I dash to the tissue box. What is this deep, old well inside me? I've just scratched the surface of something, but don't yet know exactly what or why.

When this session started, I was calm and he was upset. Somehow through this journey, we traded places. This little baby healed something and in the process I dug something up.

I decide on the most direct route home, but hit heavy traffic. "Oh, nooo!" I groan in agitation. "I've gotta get out of here!" I maneuver to the right lane so I can take the next exit. Longer? I don't care, as long as I'm not trapped in traffic. I'm an expert at back-road navigation!

Quandary

I've been crying—again. Not a day has gone by lately without this homesick feeling. Tonight I feel particularly tender. Never mind cushions and comforts, or even a box of tissues—I simply must get outside!

I sit on my cement porch, lean against the wall, pull up my knees, and watch the pure, beautiful Colorado night sky. Watching, waiting, imploring...and crying.

Arcturus, Hercules, the Northern Cross, little Delphinus, and Vega—brilliant in Lyra—all feel like my friends. After all, constellations are my specialty on the volunteer astronomy team.

But tonight is different. Tonight my quandary overtakes me: *why am I here? No, really—I don't just mean a fluffy, existential why am I here? I mean where is the star bus that dropped me off here and why has it not come to whisk me back already? My home is out there, in the big, beautiful, black cosmos of endless possibility! My soul-self belongs out there in some place of beautiful bliss, love, camaraderie, and delicious peace.*

I remember that place. *But how did I get here to Earth? I don't want to be here! What a ridiculous place—everyone is stupid, it's all about money and survival, everything is overwhelming. Sights, sounds, smells, people, annoyances—this world seems over-stimulating and confusing. People can't be trusted—well, except for some close friends and family. The good isn't worth the bad, and I'm always stressed out!*

The world is a scary, dangerous, overwhelming place, and it's unsafe simply to be alive! Life itself here threatens my survival, let alone my well being!

That's my home, I inform the stars through my tears, *that's my home out there! Please, tell me, how do I get out of here?*

Remembrance

"Mom, I know I was born via C-section, but why?" In my infant development training we'd been exploring the beneficial effects of the baby's journey through the birth canal.

"Your head was stuck back," Mom replies.

"You mean when I was trying to come out?"

"Yeah, my contractions started and got closer together—but then got further apart. They took an x-ray and saw that your head was tilted backward and you couldn't get out, so they did an immediate C-section."

Again I feel that gut-buzz.

"And then what?"

"They kept you in the nursery. They brought you to me to nurse," Mom recalls, "but I wasn't in good shape. You were ready to come home before I was."

What's up with this buzzing? I'm a highly sensitive person and a somatic practitioner, and decide it's time to investigate.

I go off by myself. *Okay,* I ask, *what do I notice—without judgment?* My body feels tight in a squished way. My breathing is shallow. The buzziness—adrenaline—it feels like something needs to happen *now*. I'm alone and don't feel safe. I look around for possible options of exit.

Why do I want to get out of this room—in this moment of reflection—when I don't really want to go anywhere else? I realize that my modus operandi has always been an urgent *how do I get out of here?* I've been afraid of the world—worried, anxious, and unconfident.

I've never been suicidal, just always looking for *how—how do I get off this planet?*

Well, there it is: how do I get out of this womb?

I laugh out loud. It's what I teach others: *birth matters!* We remember—maybe not through explicit memory of the occasion, but our cells remember. Our birth experience often sets the tone for the rest of our lives.

My feelings of constant threat, overwhelm, distrust, and the deep need to know an exit plan come from my birth! This is old, early patterning. Emergency surgery and a nursery stint saved my life, but I met the world with a heightened sense of stress. My nervous system set-up was fight-or-flight mode from the start!

Mostly flight, I muse. Even my enormous love of executing back flips in the swimming pool as a kid revealed my unconscious attempts to figure out birth!

I continue to guide myself. Next, how to find a pathway from this habitual feeling to another more satisfying option? I pay attention to my breath. *There's nowhere else to go, nothing else to do,* I tell myself. *Simply be here.* This place of *just being* lives somewhere in my cells—in the consciousness each individual cell possesses.

I tap into this wisdom and feel the slowness of presence melt through my limbs. Then I go back to the stuck feeling. Then back to the free *being* place. It takes some practice, but I find out how to go from one feeling to the other. Now I have a way out.

Wise Me

"You're amazing and wonderful, and I'm so glad you're here!" I say, returning five-week-old Riley's gaze.

Birth stories come up often in my work with babies and parents. Babies automatically begin to self-heal when listened to and given the support to do so—I see this over and over again. They tell their story and release stress through crying, and they illustrate their experiences through their movements.

Once they express themselves—with our loving attention—they become more confident, peaceful, deeply joyful, and intensely relational. A baby truly heard and respected takes up her space in a very empowered way.

After seeing this happen consistently I figure I must be like that too, in the essence of my being. Can I take up my space and live empowered? I decide to try it out for myself.

"I am amazing and wonderful, and I'm so glad I'm here!" It takes practice, but I am sincere.

Baby Riley, you have something to say and want to be heard? So do I. You heal because you have this wisdom already inside yourself and you know exactly what you need. I am wise, I heal, and I know exactly what I need, too.

By simply being themselves and attempting to heal their own experiences, these babies have helped me heal. Closed down and afraid, I found a way to open up to life again. In turn, I can now support babies and their parents even more deeply.

Now I live in wonder, beauty, and safeness. No longer afraid of the world, I'm more confident. I love. I explore life with gusto. I am present. Life is not a threat! I have everything I need already inside myself, and when I get overwhelmed, I know what to do.

We remember. Our cells know, our habits give clues, and our life tells our birth story.

ABOUT THE AUTHOR: A certified Infant Developmental Movement Educator, Aware Parenting Instructor, *Body-Mind Centering®* Practitioner, spiritual counselor, and trained *Feldenkrais®* practitioner, Eliza respects babies as whole people who enter the world knowing how to communicate, learn, and self-heal. Her *Conscious Baby* practice employs a unique approach to natural "I can do it myself" milestone development and attunement to non-verbal cues and crying. Eliza's life-changing perspectives and respectful solutions toward common parenting questions transcend "typical" parenting advice. Her work addresses babies on the "well baby" spectrum *and* those experiencing challenges such as motor delay, difficulty in tummy time, and hip dysplasia.

Eliza Parker
www.ConsciousBaby.com
www.facebook.com/ConsciousBabyBlog
Eliza@ConsciousBaby.com

Christmas Past, Present, And Future

Sue Urda

Christmas Past

It's two weeks before Christmas and I haven't bought a single present, baked a single cookie, or made a single ravioli or pierogi. I don't even have any ideas for presents because I haven't allowed myself to think about it. I mean, c'mon, why think about buying gifts if there's no money to buy them with?

I haven't gone to visit my mom in Texas for the holidays because I haven't had enough money to buy a plane ticket – and this year is no different. Even though she doesn't say a word, I can feel her disappointment. Or is it mine? It doesn't matter because either way this feeling sucks!

Twelve nieces and nephews, two brothers and two sisters and their spouses, mom, Kathy and my in-laws—this is my family list for gifts. And what about my friends? What about my co-workers and all the people I'd like to recognize with even a small token of appreciation and love?

The thing is I really love the whole Christmas gift-giving process. I love finding the perfect gift, wrapping it with pretty paper and making fancy bows. I love singing along with the Christmas music as I bake buttery cookies and create sweet candies. I love the way it feels to pack the packages and mail them out.

Thank you, we loved the gift and the snowball cookies were delicious! These notes and phone calls are perhaps the best part of the experience.

Years past, we always pulled off the financial thing: a big order or a bunch of little ones, and one year we even received an unexpected and generous gift of money. Or I got a new Visa or store credit card so we could charge it all. So what if it cost 13.99% extra over time, at least we could buy gifts for Christmas.

Maybe the best part was that no one would find out the extent to which we were struggling with money. I don't think I could bear that.

Geesh, could we use a break right about now! Having started three businesses over the past twenty-five years, I know it takes time and investment capital for growth and success but my patience is running out.

I remind myself *again* that we've always been taken care of. Over the years, even the past three that have been particularly sparse, I can see that although we just barely eked it out—and often at the last minute—somehow, some way, we always pulled it off.

Money showed up in some form or other and we could pay our car insurance or electric bill just before the shut off date. And we always found the perfect Christmas solution, even if it was in the final days so gifts could be shipped via Priority Mail to arrive on December 24th.

The Universe always provided for us. Always—no exceptions.

I knew in my heart that this year would be no different, but for some reason I was stressing about it way more than usual.

Sick And Tired

The truth is I'm sick and tired of this–literally sick and tired. Sick and tired of eking it out at the last minute. Sick and tired of compromising on the perfect gifts because money's not there. Sick and tired of not seeing my family and friends because of *lack of moolah* to travel, to go on vacation, or even to go out to dinner.

It always came back to money. Or was it the other way around?

Maybe I wasn't sick and tired because I didn't have money; maybe I didn't have money because I was sick and tired.

My physical body had been on a journey of its own. Since being diagnosed with the autoimmune disease Lupus a few years ago after having had symptoms for more than ten years, I have had three periods of intense physical crisis. Maybe, just maybe, the disease held the answer to my financial crisis too.

Autoimmune diseases cause the immune system to malfunction and instead of only attacking germs, diseases or viruses, it also attacks healthy tissues and organs. Basically the body goes haywire and attacks itself.

Perhaps me not having money was me attacking and sabotaging myself.

Heck, I was smart enough and driven enough. I had creative ideas and worked long hours. And I could write a plan for business growth and financial success that would surely bring in boatloads of cash. In fact, I'd written and worked on plenty over the years with my dad and Kathy—with some pretty good results.

The manufacturing businesses brought in some pretty impressive sales, and our women's network had experienced some wonderful growth in the first five years. The intrinsic community, empowerment, and soul-filling aspects of the business worked beautifully. We were fulfilling our mission to empower and connect women and the feedback we got was terrific.

But where was the money?

Here I sit, two weeks before Christmas worrying about the money.

Christmas Present

Fast forward and I sit in amazement at the major shifts that have transpired since that desperate, definitive Christmas. I hear *Silent Night* that my neighbor whistles as he opens his front door and the jingle bells hanging from his door knob ring out. The spritz cookie I love so much drops crumbs on my chest as I take another bite and sip amaretto. It tastes just like Christmas!

So, what changed? Me. There was the deep introspection, hours and hours of walking on the beach in meditation and breathing in the bounty of life. There were pages and pages of lists of what I'm grateful for, and long talks with supportive and loving friends who have been with me on this journey over the years. Shelves filled with books new and old are marked up with lessons on self-love, self-worth, faith, healing, success, relationships and more.

I'm no longer in a funk.

I climbed out of the rut of despair and am filled with hope and exuberance. Content and happy knowing that I'm always taken care of, there's now enough money to know our future is bright.

All is well—I feel it deep in my soul. Feeling comforted and secure, I feel blessed to know that we will never be in the same financially stressed position again. I reflect on the past few years...

I explored the possibility of the sick and tired connection to the lack of financial flow, and am reminded of the teachings of Louise Hay and her amazing book, *You Can Heal Your Life*. I had relied heavily on her teachings of self-love during my first physical body crisis.

Over and over I watched the DVD of the same name as I soaked in a hot bath each day. Affirmations written on post-it notes were affixed to my bathroom mirror, and I repeated them as I drifted off to sleep in the only chair I found comfortable, as my body was wracked with pain. I prayed over healthy, nourishing foods as I cooked and ate, and I blessed my supplements and my healers.

Homeopathic and holistic therapies helped to nurse and heal me over the course of five months. The crux of my healing though was a heart and mindset adjustment and a shift in consciousness—these made the real difference in my return to health.

I had learned to love myself—to know that I am worthy and deserving of good health, a faithful body, and the love and support of others. It felt okay to not know what's coming next, and to trust that somehow, in some way, we're always taken care of. Relaxing into whatever was here for me was becoming more natural, and the sense that life is here *for* me—for my highest and best good—was my mainstay. Yes, I had learned a lot!

Healing and truly vibrant living isn't a 'one and done' situation—it's a practice.

I pondered the past 30 years of personal development and spiritual work I had done. It showed me that life is a process that never ends. Spiritual beings are on a continuum of learning and growing, birthing and dying. We never get it done, so we can't ever get it wrong. There's always tomorrow, there's a never-ending supply of whatever we desire, and awakening continues. I know this to be true, because I've experienced it over and over.

Having pulled myself out of a sick and tired, broke and stressed out rut, I've begun to live the life I know I'm capable of, and finally, I feel worthy and deserving of all the riches of life. I know they're available to me because they're available to everyone—they're our birthright.

I gaze at the Christmas candle burning brightly and hum happily to myself, *Have a Holly Jolly Christmas,* and I know we will.

Christmas Future

The Christmas music blares, yes blares, because that's the way I like it when I'm baking six different kinds of my favorite holiday cookies. I can sing as loud as I want to and no one seems to care. I gaze contentedly at our beautiful Christmas tree twinkling with white lights, adorned with shiny, bright colored ornaments, and topped with a lighted, white angel. The presents under the tree—beautifully wrapped in shiny paper and silky ribbons—are waiting to be packed and shipped with love to our family and friends who we won't be seeing for the holidays.

I smell the cookies and know it's time to ready the next tray for baking. The raviolis, pierogis, and stuffed cabbage that we handmade last week are in the freezer and we're pretty much ready to host our family and friends on Christmas day.

There's not even an inkling of worry or barely a thought about money—except for the fact that we have plenty of it right now and the knowing that more is on the way.

Feeling physically and emotionally vibrant and strong, I no longer experience the pain, inflammation, exhaustion, anxiety, and dis-ease that had been with me for so many years. I have allowed and trained myself to relax into the present moment and to breathe in the perfection of it. No longer second guessing the divine order of the universe, I trust the faithfulness and care of God.

There may still be occasions that the money comes in at the last minute, but I no longer worry about it. I trust and have faith that it always does come in—and it does! We continue to work our big, beautiful plans for our business, and we see new pathways and joint ventures opening up before us.

The future of Christmas is bright, and I trust and have faith that all is well. And so it is.

ABOUT THE AUTHOR: Sue Urda is your *Feel Good Guidess*. She has impacted thousands of women through transformative talks and inspirational writings that teach people to embrace the power of feeling good. Sue is a two-time honoree on INC Magazine's list of the 500 Fastest-Growing Private Companies, and an award-winning and Amazon #1 bestselling author. As co-founder of Powerful You! she has connected thousands of women for business, personal and spiritual growth, and has helped 150+ women achieve their dreams of becoming a published author. Sue is a thought leader who loves assisting women to *find the feel good* and live in that space every day.

Sue Urda
Powerful You! Inc.
www.powerfulyou.com
www.sueurda.com
info@powerfulyou.com

Trust In The Divine Self

Heather Keay

The mother of three toddlers, I grab every chance I can for quiet time—even if it means walking the beach in the freezing dead of winter. This particular morning, blissfully happy for the first time in a long time, I give thanks for my children and my family as peace and gratitude surround me.

Helena! I hear suddenly and from out of nowhere.

Who the heck is Helena? I wonder.

Look up!

Why am I hearing voices? I think, startled and a bit frightened. I feel like I'm surrounded by thousands of people, and when I raise my eyes to the heavens I'm shocked to see a beautiful angelic face in the sky. Panicked, I race to my mother at work to share what's just occurred.

"Mom, now I'm hearing voices on the beach!" I blurt. "What if I'm schizophrenic?"

"You have a gift, Heather," my mother says as she looks me in the eye and reminds me of the times I've called her with similar experiences. "I know that," Mom continues, "even though we've never really discussed it." She proceeds to tell me that many in her family are gifted in this way, and reassures me I'm safe and have nothing to fear.

Afraid that this gift—dormant all these years—is about to come flooding in and change my life forever, I don't realize this is just the beginning. In the process of a huge spiritual awakening, there's no stopping it! However, I must simultaneously find a way to release my fears and embrace my gifts.

"You Have To Go On And Be Crazy—Craziness Is Like Heaven" ~ Jimi Hendrix

Since youth, I possess what I call *a knowing*—like who's calling on the phone or how a movie ends. Always sensitive and intuitive, I'd dream of situations and events, and in the days and weeks that follow they'd happen—more often than not.

I begin actually seeing spirit—full apparitions of people who have passed on—in my early twenties. They appear in my room or while I'm walking down the street, and at times I think I'm going crazy! When my boyfriend Jeff and I move in together into his small Boston apartment, I'm awakened by a little boy who runs around my bed. I rub my eyes, shake my head, and go back to sleep, writing the experience off as a dream.

I go to work and tell my best friend Moura about the Native American man who guards my bedroom door. He appears from time to time during the year I live in my Beacon Hill apartment. I learn eventually that he's a spirit guide, but at the time I have no idea if I'm in my right mind. Moura and I laugh and joke about it as we run along the Charles River.

The daily energy around me is tremendously overwhelming and manifests in many different ways. I walk into a room and *feel* the energy. I sense a thickness in certain areas and a cold breeze in others. I detect my own energy level draining when I'm around people with negative energy. Some days, I'm so fatigued it's hard to get off the couch. I have no idea why I'm so exhausted all the time for no apparent reason, until I realize I have to learn to protect myself and my energy.

Colors look brighter than usual, and I begin to see zooming light orbs and random sparks of light, which I learn are spirit lights. Light orbs begin showing up in all my photos and, as I look back at older ones, they seem always to have been there—I simply wasn't ready to see them.

As a way to cope with my new reality, I start meditating. This helps me to better understand the abilities I've always had but am beginning only now to develop. I read books about spirituality and mediumship—anything I can find related to my experiences. I take lots of spiritual classes and study with local mediums to try to understand how and why I'm a channel for spirit. I need to find a way to empower myself with knowledge so I won't go crazy!

A relatively insecure person, it's not easy for me to overcome my fears and I need time to figure it all out on my own. I want to share my gift, but am scared about peoples' reactions. I practice my mediumship on Jeff, now my husband, and my immediate family.

I begin by asking for the names of loved ones that have passed to see if I can receive messages from them. When I ask a question, the answer pops into my head, or spirit shows me something I can only describe as a movie in my mind with images that convey a specific message. I see what people look like and what they are wearing. Sometimes I even glimpse family members and what they are doing at the time I'm receiving the message. My mother gets so excited when I tell her about her mother and father, and it brings her much peace.

Gradually I begin to perform readings for friends but don't tell them they are from me. When I receive a message from spirit for someone, I relay the information but explain I heard it from a medium I met. This anonymity provides me the necessary confidence to test whether or not my gift is *real*.

Coming Out

When confident enough to discuss my gifts openly with family members, I learn that this ability runs on both sides of my family. My paternal grandmother was also a spirit medium. About a year before she passes, she begins to come to me in spirit—something I now experience regularly with people who are approaching the end of their journey and about to pass.

My grandmother sits at the end of my bed at night and talks to me about her gifts and how she passed them on to me. She apologizes for not explaining more, but assures me she will help when she passes. Now that's she's gone, she assists me with my spiritual work, and I'm more connected to her than when she was alive. Her guidance helps me tremendously with my spiritual path.

The same is true of my father who, unfortunately, was not there for me growing up. When he passes in 2000, I become highly anxious and assume it's due to his sudden death. Eventually I learn that what I'm feeling is not anxiety but rather the presence of spirit—in this case it's simply my father visiting me!

Though we did not have much of a relationship before, now we have a wonderful connection! Since his passing he gives me messages and guidance—not only for me but also for my siblings. I'll never forget his warning that my brother will be in a terrible accident. It happens just as he foretells, and through this experience—and countless others—I learn that spirit is able warn us of future events, but cannot stop them from happening. This is the most difficult aspect of my gift—possessing knowledge of the future and having to accept and trust the outcome, whatever it may be.

The Real Deal

Signs of the relevance and importance of the name *Helena* continue to present themselves. That night, when I hit the pause button while watching television to run downstairs and tell Jeff about my experience that afternoon, I see the name *Helena* displayed on the screen. Shocked, I photograph it to make sure it's not simply my imagination.

The following day my five year-old son becomes ill and we rush him to the hospital. When brought to his room, I see the name *Helena* written on his board—she's the nurse on duty. Again, I photograph it—I've never known anyone named Helena and here's that name twice in two days!

I realize someone is trying to get my attention and give me a message. I learn eventually that *Helena* is my guardian angel's name. Until that day on the beach, I'd see spirit, but now my hearing kicks in. I begin to ask for guidance and signs, and within what feels like moments I trust what I'm hearing, sensing, and seeing, which is how my angelic photography is born.

I'm given a message to look up, and every time I do there in the clouds is the clear shape of an angel, a rainbow, or a heart! I keep the photos to myself at first, but then decide they should be shared with the world because help and guidance is all around—we need only look for and be open to it.

Finally, I prove to myself that my gifts *are real.* Previously so difficult for me to come clean, I've taken years to reveal to others that *I'm* really the medium! I decide to obtain a Reiki Masters and an Advanced Level Integrated Energy Therapy certification. I want to be able to connect to divine energies to help others heal.

Eventually I take a leap of faith, "come out," and open my own healing center. I want it to be a place where I can conduct my spiritual work openly and comfortably. Often, when conducting a healing session, I receive messages from a loved one for my client and pass them on.

Still, I worry about people teasing or judging my young children if they find out about my abilities, and I worry for Jeff. What will his coworkers think? Will it affect his business? I stress about fitting in to my community. Will people think I'm weird or crazy?

Gradually I release all these fears through the support of my family and friends. Jeff has been my biggest fan from the very beginning. He likes to call me superwoman because of how I've kept hidden my talents from the outside world for so long. He's very proud of me, and who can ask for more than that? Without his support, I wouldn't be able to accomplish all the healing work I do.

Besides, what type of role model am I to my children if I hide who I really am? I can't control what people think of me! I *know* the work I do helps heal hearts, and I've changed so many peoples' lives for the better, I can't stop now! My gift's impact on clients is so beautiful—their tears of joy make it all worthwhile.

Currently writing a book that includes personal mediumship stories and my spirit photography, I hope to inspire others to believe in themselves and their own gifts. If my story helps others to embrace the gifts God has given them and to trust in the divine self, I am happy to have been of service.

ABOUT THE AUTHOR: Heather Keay is a married mother of three and lives in Cohasset, Massachusetts. She offers mediumship readings and alternative healing therapies at her practice, JLJ Healing & Wellness Center. She has her Reiki Masters and Advanced Level Integrated Energy Therapy certification. Like so many mediums I have always "known" on some level that I had a gift. The challenge was opening up to it and truly taking ownership of it, being proud of it, and using it to help others.

Heather Keay, Spirit Medium, RMT
Cohasset, MA 02025
www.jljhealing.com
heatherkeay@jljhealing.com
781-383-8444

Looking For A Miracle

Lauren Rocha

The ground opens and darkness swallows me up. At least that's what it feels like when I hear the doctor say: "Your mother has two to three months to live...I'm very sorry...there's nothing we can do..."

I stare at him in disbelief as his words register. Outside the hospital window I see people walking, talking, laughing. The sun is shining. Nothing seems to have changed, but my life will never be the same...

Later that day, I speak to my brother. He reassures me, in his usual positive manner, that statistics are not always right. I want to believe him—I *need* to believe him!

Everything happens so fast. Diagnosed with stomach cancer after a fall at the Shrine of Our Lady of Fatima in Portugal, our sixty-year-old mother undergoes emergency surgery and we receive her prognosis.

Nothing has prepared me for this! Powerless, I don't know what to do! I know only that I can't repeat the doctor's words to her. She's confident and hopeful that the surgery went well. I cannot shatter her hope!

However, neither can I simply wait and do nothing. I want a miracle, but don't believe in miracles. I've never felt the need to question my beliefs, but now I have no answers—nothing to sustain me or give me hope, no strength to carry on...

The Search Begins

My mother feels ill during a visit to the Shrine of Our Lady of Fatima where, accompanied by her four children—me and my three siblings—we have honored her request to go. We respect her Catholic faith, though none of us practice it. Catholicism doesn't make sense to any of us—we crave a more scientific understanding of how everything is connected, of how prayer works, and of the mind, body, and spirit.

For her the Shrine of Our Lady of Fatima is a miraculous place. I remember reading that Pope John Paul II affirmed he survived the assassination attempt on his life in Saint Peter's Square in 1981, because the Lady of Fatima's "unseen" and "maternal hand" miraculously rescued and saved him. Pope John Paul II later says he saw Fatima intervene and that he maintained consciousness on the ride to the hospital by keeping his mind focused on her. He becomes known as the "Fatima Pope".

My mother's fall, subsequent operation, and diagnosis awaken me to what is really precious in life. They remove her stomach and in the beginning she can't eat and is very frail. A ten year struggle ensues, during which I am aware that every celebration—every birthday—could be her last.

Her situation causes me to begin to question, to start looking for a miracle. In the process, I come across a poem entitled "the search," written when I was a school girl, that seems to exemplify my inner struggle.

the search
to hunger and thirst for more and more
to attempt to see behind the door
that promises to satisfy her need
that vows her heart to stop to bleed
what prevents her from opening this door far and wide
why does she fear when dreams have already died
what more or else does she have to lose
when all that is left is this freedom to choose
so give her your hand and guide her way
no longer hide
but beside her stay

Could it be that I was already looking for a miracle back then? Could it be that my mother's illness will help me reconnect to that young girl's spiritual search?

The Search Continues

Days go by, painfully, slowly...in my search for a miracle, I begin to read the life stories of many that experienced similar trials, and perhaps even heard the words *I'm very sorry...there's nothing we can do...*

I come across Bernie Siegel's humane and empowering book *Love, Medicine, & Miracles: Lessons Learned About Self-Healing From*

A Surgeon's Experience With Exceptional Cancer Patients. I read how courageously so many defy circumstances, survive adversities, challenge beliefs, and miraculously heal.

They use prayer, affirmations, creative visualization, and other holistic healing therapies that work for them. Above all, when they take responsibility for their own healing, the transformation in their lives is truly inspiring!

While continuing to look for a miracle, I find Louise Hay's uplifting work and her story of miraculous personal healing. I read how she's touched millions of lives and helped cure so many with her love, knowledge, and wisdom.

These extraordinary life stories become anchors that sustain me. They spur me on to continue looking for a miracle to cure my mother and myself. For I feel that I need healing too, as my yearning to wake up spiritually grows daily.

I share with my mother these miracles through the use of holistic healing therapies, but soon realize that her faith is unwavering— she's at peace with whatever happens; serene with whatever comes. I marvel at this: her faith is enough for her. Actually, her faith seems to become stronger and firmer as she faces her illness bravely.

I continue to read and learn about various healing methods. From each lesson, I take what makes sense and believe will work for me. Like the remarkable transformations of many exceptional people, the regular use of healing techniques becomes an invaluable source of support during these years of questioning, seeking, and awakening to the miraculous in life.

I become aware that my mother's illness also challenges us as a family. I find myself reassessing priorities and making changes in my life, so that what I begin to value most in life is in harmony with the person I'm becoming. Each day is a gift and a blessing for which I am grateful! I learn to appreciate more the time we spend together as a family, and we all become closer.

Perhaps one of the most valuable gifts during this healing process is becoming aware of the good that already exists in life, and being thankful for this. I realize now that I've taken so much for granted before. This experience is certainly a wake-up call!

I learn from Bernie Siegel—as I read about his exceptional cancer patients—that even though some patients aren't cured, they learn to make peace with leaving because of their belief that there's something more...

"There Are Two Ways To Live Life: One As If Nothing Is A Miracle; The Other As If Everything Is A Miracle." ~ Albert Einstein

Days, months, and years pass until fifteen years have gone by and my mother is still alive! It isn't easy. Often I feel lost, anxious, afraid, powerless. Nowadays, I pray still for serenity to accept the unavoidable parting of loved ones. I'm certain the support of family and friends helped my mother heal, but I believe, ultimately, that it's due to her faith, which—throughout the many years of fighting for her health—remains firm and unshaken.

I've learned to respect my mother's spiritual path. Her faith and healing is a source of inspiration to me. My spiritual awakening goes hand in hand with my mother's healing—for this is a story of two mothers and two daughters! Our Lady of Fatima, a spiritual mother to many believers, including us both, and *my* mother and *me*, her daughter.

In spite of the daily news of senseless loss, devastation, and grief, in the midst of my despair I come across lives that fill mine with hope, love, courage, and faith. Inspired to experience this life in a more conscious, serene, and grateful state, I owe them much for they awaken me to the miraculous in life.

I've learned also to honor my own spiritual journey and awakening, which help me see that in this life we are part of a collective consciousness and energy that unites us all. I better understand what I really value most, and awaken to the spiritual belief that there is a higher intelligence.

This experience challenges me to live more consciously. I strive daily to focus more of my energy on the good I want to create and manifest in my life. I use affirmations on a daily basis. Sometimes I say playfully that "my life has become an affirmation," for I can't perceive a day without their use, as they give purpose and meaning to my existence.

My parents gave me the precious gift of freedom to find my own spiritual path, and I'm deeply grateful to them for I know this is a privilege and a blessing. I perceive this also as a responsibility to help create a better self, as well as to contribute to the making of a healthier and kinder world. While looking for a miracle, I found an abundance of the miraculous in life!

The Leap Of Faith

I find great comfort in writing, and conclude with a recent poem that speaks of my quest for healing, for the miraculous in life, and of finding the miracle for which I was looking:

she knew there was more
she just knew there was more
she felt it in the innermost depths of her soul
she sensed it with all her power and strength
she yearned for more
she longed for better

what does she want
the big question
that she has dodged for so long
the answer she has avoided for many years
with senseless distractions

hiding in soundless voids
invisible in faceless multitudes
till the day
her need could no longer be numbed
nor her voice ignored

she listens to the yearnings of her heart
to the longings of her soul
she aspires for more and better
for herself and dear ones
for the world

the day has come
when she needs wants
the knowledge that she has tried
she has dared to take a leap of faith
into the unknown the unexplored

she hears
the urgent thumping of her heartbeat
as she searches
for answers and meaning
to make sense of life and learning

the time has come
to look beyond the walls she has created
lonesome labyrinth
binding barriers
her own self imposed limitations

to wake up
from a deep slumber
to shine at last

to let light illuminate her way
her journey every day

to feel
joy when the sun comes up
gratitude when she goes to sleep
blissful serenity
wholesome reality

to embrace
the gigantic web called life
immersed in enlightened energy
to help create
a better self a better world

to see
with her soul
listen with her heart
feel what she cannot touch
to be one with the infinite creative self

this is her passion
her dream
her aspiration
her answer
her voice

for she knew there was more
there was better

ABOUT THE AUTHOR: Lauren Rocha graduated in Literature, and has been a language teacher for nearly twenty years. She's particularly interested in the rich diversity of learners' styles, and in making the learning process an enjoyable and enriching experience. She enjoys spending time with family and friends, reading and writing, learning about holistic therapies, and going for long walks in nature. She has taken the Louise Hay's 'Heal your Life' training, is a certified NLP practitioner, and author of a poetry book, 'oh yes to the magic pen'.

Lauren Rocha
Rua da Agrela, 52, Serzedo,
4405-090 Vila Nova de Gaia, Portugal
laurirenti@gmail.com
(+351) 910059721

Swinging My Way Through

Kathy Fyler

So excited and nervous all at once, I've been dreaming of playing golf again for what seems like forever, and here I am at the first hole. The toughest on the course...so much anticipation.

"I'll go first" I said to Sue thinking *I got this*.

I take out my driver and a shiny new pink golf ball. I pull on my bright white leather glove and tighten the Velcro strap. Stretching my back a little as I breathe in the freshness of the newly cut grass, I take a few random, slow swings.

Carefully, I place the ball on the tee at what I remember to be the perfect height.

I'm ready, I think to myself and step forward to address the ball. As I square for the stroke I physically prepare myself–shift the weight on my feet back and forth, bend at the knees, one arm straight and the other slightly bent, head down, loose at the waist. *Okay, now I'm ready.*

I gently pull the club back and swing it forward with some speed. Feeling good as the club strikes the ball, I look into the sky ahead of me to follow the arc of my shot. *Where is it?* I look down to the tee in front of me and see my pretty pink ball sitting only two feet away. *How embarrassing. What was it about this game that I missed?*

Connection

In my twenties I played golf a few times a month. It was a great way to spend time with my mom, my friends, and even the women from work. Golf is a game you can play with pretty much anyone and the skill level does not have to be even.

My mom and I played at a local 9-hole course and we would walk instead of use a golf cart. There was one hole where we would tee off from a mini cliff and it reminded me of the scenery of Tortola in the British Isles—a place our family had vacationed—so we nicknamed it the "The Tortola Hole". It was a difficult hole because of the large pond situated between the tee and the green. Often, we both hit our balls into the water. Most times we would laugh it off, get out another ball, and start the hole over again.

I also was able to play with my Uncle Jim. He was both a fun and funny man, and he belonged to a country club where he once took me to play. It was the first time that I played on an exclusive course. The grass was so green and velvety that it felt like walking on a soft, plush carpet. The greens were manicured—smooth and fast. All the holes were tree-lined and had great shrubs too, and I felt like I was in a park—all by myself! I fell in love with the beauty and opulence of it all.

In my thirties and forties, I didn't play much golf—I was "busy" building my career and my life, so I didn't make time for it any more. It was something that always made it to my vision board, bucket list, and wish list—just never to my schedule. Also, living in the northeast limited the amount of days available for playing golf—either it was rainy, cold and snowy or too hot and muggy.

After moving to Florida almost three years ago, I finally began to play again. Since my parents moved here too, I often play with both of them, and sometimes even my brother. It's a great way to spend time and bond with the family.

It wasn't until I started playing again that I realized one of the main reasons I love golf—it's the connection that it provides. Connection to the people that I want to be around and have a relationship with. Connection to nature—the sun, the ground, the trees, the birds, the fresh air. These things feed my soul. This sense of connection allows my mind to open to spirit and be at peace. It makes me feel at one with those I love.

Golf is a meditation for me.

The Present Moment

Playing golf has many times, strike that, *oftentimes* tried my patience. Sure there are those times that I go out on the course and seamlessly hit the ball so it lands where I want it to, but most times this is not the case.

When I'm not playing well I have to remind myself to stop, take a deep breath in and return to my mantra "Head down, follow through". This helps to ground me and get me back on track.

Sometimes it takes a few strokes to get back in the swing of things, but with my mantra I get there.

There have also been times on the course where a foursome in front of us seemed to take all the time in the world to make their shots, and it called for patience to wait for them. Other times, a twosome behind us seemed to be in such a hurry and it felt like they were hitting their shots before I was even finished with my swing.

To enjoy the game for fully, I had a choice to make—ask the foursome if we could "play through", allow the twosome to go ahead of us, or I could simply focus on myself, my shot, my golf partners and the surrounding beauty. The choice is mine.

My favorite time to play golf is in the early to late afternoon. This is the least busy time to play, because most players are finishing their last few holes and are heading to the nineteenth hole—the clubhouse bar. There is something soothing about being on the course as the day is ending and the sun is beginning to set.

Is it possible that being on the golf course makes me feel closer to God? It is for me.

Intuition

Standing on the green, I bend down to prepare for my putt. I check the lie of the green, the gentle slope of ground, and the distance to the hole. I know that my touch, speed and the angle of my putter matters. I know that I'm not an expert at reading the greens because I haven't had much practice. I also know that it doesn't matter that much.

I've developed a "sense" for exactly what to do. Sure, I use the technical skills that I've learned from watching the pros on TV, watching some YouTube videos, and from my experience, but all of these pale in comparison to being in the flow and allowing my intuition guide me.

Some of my best shots happened when I simply "felt" my way through, gave myself over to the moment, and struck with abandon.

Every golfer knows that it doesn't matter if it's the first time playing a course or the tenth—each time the course plays differently, and every shot sets you up in a new way. Starting from your first drive, you never, ever land in the exact same spot on the fairway, and hopefully you've at least made it to the fairway and not in a sand trap, a water hazard, or the rough.

Each shot determines your next move. Wherever your ball lands on the course, you have lots of decisions to make—which club to use, how to set up for your shot, and how hard to swing. For me, feeling my way through has been a lifesaver—and a game saver.

I use the same approach off the course, like when we decided to move to Florida. Our decision to move "south" seemed natural for us. The year-round warmer weather sounded great, as did the opportunity for a "kickstart" for our business.

We've rented vacation condos over the internet in the past and have always been pleased with the accommodations, but renting a place to live year-round, sight-unseen was new to us. After an intense search, I finally connected with a landlord of a condo in beautiful Marco Island, FL, a place that we had visited for only one day many years ago. Ken was so helpful and friendly, and the pictures looked pretty good too, but what were we really getting into? We'd find out when we arrive.

The anticipation for our move grew, and then moving day came. We packed up the U-Haul trailer that was hitched to our SUV and headed south. We drove happily on I-95 and crossed the border to Georgia when suddenly the car started to decelerate.

Slower and slower we moved until finally we were able to pull to the side of the highway. The engine ceased. *What's happening?*

AAA arrived a full 75-minutes after we called, because it was a Sunday and we were pretty much in the middle of nowhere. We had some time to ponder our situation.

Thirty degrees when we left New Jersey two days ago, it was now a muggy ninety degrees at two-thirty in the afternoon. What were we thinking? Was this the right move? Maybe the Universe was trying to tell us something—like turn back!

The mechanic arrived and towed us to a local AutoZone (no service stations were opened because it was Sunday), and a very kind, knowledgeable, and helpful clerk discovered that we had simply run out of oil.

You're kidding! I had a nudge to check this before we left, but in our hurry, I ignored it. I know better than to ignore my nudges. I know my intuition is on target, and this was simply another reminder.

Feeling Good

Birds are singing, a light breeze blows through my hair, and the sun warms my body with morning rays. My pretty pink ball sails in a beautiful arc through the air, lands squarely on the fairway and rolls ahead another twenty yards. Ahhhh... this feels good!

I have learned that golf is not just a physical game; it is a game of the mind and heart.

Having set my intention to have a great round, I'm able to engage the ball with the ease of a pro—not the score of a pro, but the ease and confidence of a pro.

I relax into my swing, take time to feel the club in my hands, breathe deeply and repeat my mantra, "Head down, follow through". I am one with the ball.

The connection of golf to my everyday life does not escape me. I know that however I feel shows up in my long-term results and in each moment. I remind myself to feel good as I swing my way through life.

ABOUT THE AUTHOR: Kathy's earlier career includes being a Critical Care Nurse, Project Manager for a technology firm, and owner of a $5 million manufacturing company. In 2005, Kathy followed her calling to make "more of a contribution to what matters most in this world". Using her experience and passion for technology and people, she co-founded Powerful You! Women's Network and Powerful You! Publishing to fulfill her personal mission of assisting women in creating connections via the internet, live meetings and the published word. Kathy is an Amazon #1 Bestselling Author who loves to travel the country connecting with and teaching women.

Kathy Fyler
Co-Founder of Powerful You! Inc.
www.powerfulyou.com
www.powerfulyoupublishing.com
info@powerfulyou.com

The *Real* Story

Sheri Horn Hasan

Damn, why can't I get up off this frickin' couch and go for a walk? Why am I so exhausted? Yeah, I know I have multiple sclerosis, but sheesh, I lost my excess weight nearly ten years ago now and have been walking for exercise ever since—what's the matter with me?

My inner critic insists on berating me—sometimes I'm a beached whale, other times simply lazy—but no matter what, I continue not to be able to move.

It's important for me to move because, since my MS diagnosis I've kept my weight down through regular walking—hardly anything I'd call athletic, but enough to keep me healthy and able to control any excess caloric intake. A Taurus Sun, I do love my food!

Having been bitten by the astrology bug a few years before, I consult my astrology books for answers.

"This is not a time to strike out to further your own self interest in life," writes Robert Hand in Planets In Transit. "Your energy level is low and you are subject to fits of discouragement and malaise."

He's talking about transiting Neptune coming up to (conjoining) my natal Mars in Aquarius in my sixth house of health, work, and service. I've seen this coming and dread it because I don't know exactly how it will affect me.

I know the planet Mars in our charts represents our initiative, both physical and mental—especially physical. In archetypal terms, Mars represents motivation, ambition, assertion, aggression, sexuality, and—when taken to an extreme—violence. Mars likes to leap, not to lie about like a beached walrus!

Meanwhile, the planet Neptune bears an archetypal energy that ranges from one's connection to the mystical, spiritual, and divine to that of illusion, confusion, and delusion. Put another way, Neptune's energy is not of the body, and can manifest as the height of spirituality or martyrdom in some, or as addictive behavior in others.

"This is one of the more difficult transits of Neptune, because the nature of Mars and that of Neptune are very much opposed to each other," Hand continues. "Mars in your horoscope stands for your ego drives, but Neptune manages to pull the rug out from under them.

"Mars makes you assert your individuality and take the necessary actions to establish your place in the world among other people. Whatever you do along these lines—working to get ahead in your job, beginning a new enterprise, or embarking on a new program of vigorous mental or physical activity—Neptune will make it difficult for you to succeed."

What? Oh, great! I just received a contract to edit the Powerful You! Publishing book! A former journalist, book editing is new to me, and I'm a tad nervous.

"Even if you want to do something, you may just feel too tired," Hand adds, hammering the metaphorical nail into my psychological coffin.

C'mon, I thought I fought this demon already and had it beat! In the early days of my diagnosis, fatigue was my overwhelming symptom. I learned, little by little, how to say no to engaging in activities that depleted my energy with little or no return.

It wasn't easy, but day by day, week by week, month by month, I regained my strength and energy by walking two miles as many days per week as my energy—and my schedule—would allow. Now, however, walking is the last thing on earth I want to do! Just the thought of getting up from my chair, or couch, or bed, fatigues me!

"...Neptune has a dissolving or clouding effect on Mars," writes Howard Sasportas in his brilliant book The Gods Of Change. "We feel lethargic and listless or unsure of what direction to take. Even if we have a sense of what it is we want to do, we could have great difficulty motivating ourselves and getting started."

Forget it, I think, as I surrender to my seemingly unwarranted physical exhaustion. I'll try again tomorrow...

Yeah, right, my helpful inner critic one-two punches me, tomorrow—when you'll be peppy—like today—yeah, right...

Through The Looking Glass

Poised on the diving board of a neighbor's above ground pool, I place my nine-year-old hands together above my head and lean forward, just as I've been taught that year in my swimming lessons at the Jewish Community Center.

I'm bravely wearing my brand spanking new green two piece

bathing suit, and about to dive into the pool, when suddenly one of the kids from the neighborhood points at me and shouts:

"Look out, the whale's jumping in the pool!"

All heads swivel to look at me. Devastated, I don't know what to do! Caught like a deer in the headlights, I hesitate, then dive in. As I surface from the water, I hear them laughing still.

Weight is an issue for me. As far back as I can remember, my mother tries to push food on my skinny older brother, Phil. Whatever he refuses I volunteer to eat.

"Not you," my mother admonishes me. "Phil is the one who's too skinny—he needs to gain weight, not you!" The only food I don't like is peas and carrots, but it's one of the few foods Phil eats. So I give him all of mine, then ask for seconds on spaghetti, potatoes, rice, you name it—the starchier, the better!

It doesn't help that my parents aren't exactly skinny themselves. My dad sports thirty extra pounds, and my mom—who has the misfortune of being only four-feet-eleven-inches tall—is forever battling her weight. None of us qualify as obese, but no one will ever mistake any of us for thin. Except for Phil, of course...

Neither does it help that my family is particularly sedentary, except—of course—for Phil! He seems to have a faster metabolism. That's a word that's used a lot in my household while growing up—metabolism—and clearly my brother's is naturally faster than mine.

I don't mind, we're different and that's ok with me. What I don't like is how I stack up against the girls my age. You know, the thin ones...I look in the mirror periodically and try to imagine myself skinny.

One night I actually have a dream that a tiny green Martian comes down to earth in a spaceship like one I'd see on the television cartoon show The Jetsons. Holding a special ray gun, he offers to zap me with it, which will cause all of my excess weight to disappear.

Yay, I'll be "normal" like the other girls! I jump at the chance!

Needless to say, I wake up quite disappointed...

Archetypal Reawakening

It's all good, I think, I've got plenty of work to do, and none of it is physically taxing! I begin work on Empowering Transformations For Women—Powerful You! Publishing's first anthology of women's short memoir stories. I receive my first draft stories and begin to edit.

As I read through them, I realize in a flash of intuition that several authors attempt to do what I call "write around the story."

In other words, they've written everything but the actual story and present a partial story in only the vaguest of terms.

I accrue more manuscripts, and notice that some stories allude to sexual abuse or manipulation, others skirt the issues of parental negligence or abuse, and still more leave out large chunks of connecting information that prevent the reader from actually understanding the full story's point.

I begin to call upon my early studies of literature and remember that the main goal of all creativity—be it through writing, film, art, music, etc.—is to create catharsis, or an emotional release by members of an audience. Slowly it dawns on me that authors are writing about the major themes in literature I learned while obtaining my B.A. in English: man vs. man, man vs. God, and man vs. nature.

Throughout my studies—from junior high school through college— I've been fascinated with archetypes and how they form the basis for the hero's journey. Joseph Campbell coined this term to describe how the path of the lives of many protagonists, or characters, in great works of literature follow a particular pattern. The archetype of the hero's journey is present in all great literature, from religious stories (including the Bible) to Greek tragedy, to modern novels and memoirs.

My knowledge of these archetypes—enhanced through my more recent study of psychological and evolutionary astrology—allows me to pinpoint directly and easily the major archetypal theme of any given author's story and to guide them intuitively. So much so that many authors, astounded at my intuitive capabilities, thank me profusely for helping them better understand the true meanings behind their stories.

Between Heaven And Earth

Time goes by and, as I receive additional stories to edit, I continue to berate myself for my physical laziness. Desperate still to figure out why I can't raise my energy level higher, I seek a better explanation of how this Neptune transit to my Mars is supposed to serve me.

Since I believe all astrological events related to my individual birth chart provide me with opportunities to grow in consciousness, I continue to seek salvation through explanation.

"Any transit of Neptune to Mars will alter the manner in which we assert ourselves..." Sasportas writes. If we use "...our drive and energy to promote something which will not only benefit us, but which will serve others in some way, then these transits do not have to yield such disastrous consequences.

"Neptune wants us to relinquish using our Mars...for our own ends...we are being asked to give away our power, and to employ it to help others rather than just ourselves. In this way we have raised Mars to a 'higher' level, because we are exercising our personal will for the good of others."

I smile wryly at his use of the word exercise. However, I take his words to heart and hope begins to blossom.

The sixth house of health, everyday routine, and service, is ruled naturally by the planet Mercury's sign of Virgo. Neptune here is not "concerned with helping others in the ordinary sense," explains astrologer and Jungian analyst Liz Greene in The Astrological Neptune, "for it is not others we serve; it is God or the gods, whose nature is best expressed through those tasks and skills which embody divine meaning."

This work is that of "building bridges between heaven and earth," and "is not always...conscious in the individual," Greene concludes.

Suddenly it dawns on me: Holy moly! This transit is asking me to let go of working for any purely selfish interest...I'm being asked to help channel the creative power of others!

Relieved when this transit finally passes after the completion of my editing work, I regain my energy once again. Grateful for this, I'm thrilled by my newfound "talent" to easily intuit an authors' true theme and help her express the real story!

ABOUT THE AUTHOR: Amazon #1 Bestseller author and editor Sheri Horn Hasan has worked with 150+ published authors to help bring their memoir stories to life. An editor for *Powerful You! Publishing's* four anthologies of women's short stories, Sheri guides authors to identify their major theme(s), *show* rather than tell, structure their story, and create catharsis with their reading audience to create unforgettable written work! A former trade journalist and editor, and professional psychological & archetypal astrologer Sheri uses her knowledge of literature, mythology, and the archetypes to help authors hone in on how to best write, organize, structure, and perfect their manuscripts.

Sheri Horn Hasan
Karmic Evolution Editorial & Publishing Services, LLC
www.KarmicEvolution.com
Sheri@KarmicEvolution.com
732-547-0852

The Vicious Circle

Jennifer Bradshaw Almond

A single black silk shirt remains in the closet—the one I gave to my best friend Karen because she loved it so much that I wanted her to have it.

"How the hell did I get here?" I cry as I fall to my knees. I stare at the blouse as a steady stream of tears flow down my face. The hardwood floors of my newly purchased house support my empty body.

How the hell did I get here? is the only thought that comes to mind as I sit slumped over—consumed with grief, betrayal, sadness, and darkness—on the floor of the room where Karen had slept.

"I wanted her to have my shirt, not my husband!" I cry. I pick up the phone to call my mom, but realize there's no way for me to reach her, and begin to wail in agony. *All I want is to be held by my mom, but God has taken her away from me in my deepest, darkest time of need!* This thought leads to more tears...

Mourning for my mom makes me want to call Jeff, my husband. This leads to a lack of oxygen to my lungs. Trapped in a vicious circle of deep dark aloneness and grief, I look at myself on the floor. I'm 265 pounds—the heaviest I've ever been—and just turned thirty.

I've done everything I should to have this perfect life, and now I have to start all over again—by myself—completely alone with no idea how to do it by myself!

Best Friends Or Worst Enemies?

The best of friends, Karen and I meet when I'm fourteen and a freshman in high school. She's two years older than me, but we really hit it off. Karen lets me drive her car before I even have my driver's license, and I learn to love country music as we cruise around.

We pass notes in school as we travel the halls. I end up attending

Virginia Tech after visiting her one weekend, though originally I had no intention of staying in Virginia for college. Being able to be with Karen is somehow very comforting.

Inseparable in college, she helps edit my papers and advises me about what classes and professors to take. We attend business school together to study management, both join the marching band, and she's present when I meet Jeff and we begin to date.

We remain good friends after college, and our families even vacation together. A huge part of my life, she supports me in anything and everything I do—and I do the same.

She's at my mom's bedside for the last moments of her life. True best friends, we celebrate the good times and support each other through the bad.

Jeff and I buy our first townhouse six months after my mom's passing. Finally financially stable enough to purchase a home, we find our starter house nestled in the woods that back up to a peaceful park yet only a couple miles from Reston Towne Center.

There's so much space in our new home that when Karen decides to leave her husband, there's no way I can allow her to move back into her childhood home—the one she hated in high school. I talk it over with Jeff and we decide to invite her to move in with us until she can figure out what to do next.

I'm still grieving and know that having Karen here will be so comforting, I think. She moves in and proves to be not only a comfort but a distraction from my grief.

Soon Jeff begins working late and Karen starts to stay at her parents' house more often, despite how odd that seems to me. In July, Jeff doesn't come home at all. Instead, his mother calls asking me to keep the challenges we're having under wraps.

Confused about what "challenges" she means, I realize she knows more than she's telling me. Since Jeff won't come home, I begin to put together phone calls from the phone bills and compare them to my calendar appointments when I was out seeing friends or visiting my dad. That's when I realize his phone was calling Karen's phone and vice versa.

His mother's cryptic clues finally make sense and lead me to confirm my worst suspicion—that Jeff and Karen are having an affair!

What's Best For Jenn?

In my deepest darkest moments I run—away from everything I

know. For months I travel on weekends to various states and cities nowhere near my home to see different friends. The last place I want to be is in this house.

I buy myself a new car, a deep blue Jeep Wrangler with a soft top so I can take it down and feel the wind in my hair. Amped up tires raise me high above the road and give me the elevated confidence I lack as a result of the deceit and betrayal that have ripped through my soul.

The emotional struggle of attempting to let go of the hurt and pain I feel from losing Jeff—combined with missing my mom—send me spiraling into a very vicious circle. When I miss Jeff, I want my mom, but she's not here; when I miss my mom, I want Jeff, and he isn't here! In between I pour my emotions and energy into dreaming of a new relationship...

Eventually I stop running and start sitting with all that I think and feel. Only then do I begin to awaken to the fact that I've spent much of my time taking care of everyone but myself. Now it's time to figure out what's best for Jenn! For the past thirty years I didn't think about this—I didn't have the tools.

So I stop running and dedicate my time to taking care of *me*. Now my focus, after all this traveling and reflection, is on taking care of my mind, body—and most of all—my spirit. To do this I still need an outlet, and I turn this energy I feel about others into inward energy to fuel my spirit. In my deepest darkest moments I remember my devotion and find my faith in God and in myself.

One of the first things I realize is that there's no one to take care of financial matters but me, so I need a second job. I find part-time employment as a greeter at the local gym where I escape during the week in order to avoid going home to an empty house.

Meeting and greeting new people as they come in to work out is a good distraction because I'm able to feel comfortable in conversation here. The gym becomes a place I go to for community, and where I sit in reflection and prayer.

The gym also turns out to be the way to help quiet my mind, and peace begins to come to me when I exercise. The more I work out, the more I actually begin to feel alive again. This becomes my sanctuary, and I feel my energy transmute right there on the gym floor as I transform my body and my mind...

I start to see beauty and grace in the things around me once again. I learn to have gratitude for all things, and especially for the people in my life. I'm invigorated by my newfound respect for my body and my ability to live free again. I begin to see the challenges in my life were actually necessary lessons to help rebuild my soul's foundation.

Life is continuing on and I'm not afraid of that, I write in my journal. *I recognize that I can't do this on my own, but am on the right track to heal, accept myself, believe in myself and—most importantly—give myself wholly to God.*

"Life Ain't Always Beautiful But It's A Beautiful Ride." ~ Gary Allan

When I begin to really practice self-love, everything starts to change. I lose almost ninety pounds, make new friends, and start living again. I learn to make choices that feel good and help me heal. I even begin to teach others what I've learned by becoming a personal trainer and group fitness instructor.

It's amazing the things I have discovered about myself, I write in my journal. *The exciting thing about it is to have someone with whom to share these thoughts and beliefs. The sucky thing is to wait to have that person find me—if I am ever found by another man on this earth. God's plan may not be for me to have another person find me, but I hope and want it to be so...*

What things have I learned about myself? I have learned patience is a good thing and so is perseverance. To believe in God is truly the way to feel free and not alone. I have learned how to be vulnerable and not regret too much. And I'm slowly able to let go and establish boundaries.

I've learned to enjoy working out to better my health, and not to feel guilty about the things that are there to protect me or help make me better. I've learned to appreciate my body and mind more. Although my mind thinks way too much, I've needed to exercise my newly discovered self-discipline and not let my mind get away from me."

Heartbreaking betrayal and deceit taught me to love myself more and to take better care of what I need and desire. It taught me also to really deepen into what my desires are, who I want to be, and to stop trying to be someone I think others want me to be. Now I know that the first step in loving myself more is to take care of the physical body that houses my spirit.

I know now that no matter where I go I am not alone. God is with me and is in everything; God makes everything enjoyable. I realize now that searching for love and validation on the outside leaves me feeling only more alone and abandoned. The key for me is to find my answers within by learning to love my body, my mind, and my emotions.

Eventually, as my body shrinks, my faith increases, and my self-love expands, my career grows and I fall in love with Greg, now my second husband. I know now that reawakening to my faith in God and myself is what helps break the vicious circle. Taking care of myself and choosing the higher road reminds me I am whole and helps me to live a more fulfilling and happier life.

ABOUT THE AUTHOR: Certified Holistic Health Coach, Kinesiologist, and Registered Yoga Teacher, Jenn draws on her own life experiences to support women through personal discovery to nurture their body in order to live life to the fullest. A natural confidant and loving individual, Jenn is a teacher at heart and encourages women to explore all aspects of holistic health and heal from the inside out. She uses her intuition to guide women through their transformation of revolutionary healing. Jenn resides in the great woodlands of Middleburg, VA with her husband, Greg and enjoys traveling, reading, playing outdoors and connecting with family and friends.

Jennifer Bradshaw Almond
Personal Wellness Revolution
www.personalwellnessrevolution.com
jenn@personalwellnessrevolution.com
703-474-5244

About the Authors

Are you inspired by the stories in this book?
Let the authors know.

See the contact information at the end of each chapter
and reach out to them.

They'd love to hear from you!

Author Rights & Disclaimer

Acknowledgements & Gratitude

First and foremost, we are grateful for the inspired and inspiring women who share their stories in these pages. Your courage, resilience, and love shine through in your words, and you're a beautiful example for women everywhere who seek to live a life that is uniquely their own. The way is now lit, the path forged, and you are leading the way! Faith, passion and purpose are your hallmark and we honor each of you with deep respect and love.

We have deep appreciation for the experts who have helped to birth this book: our editor Sheri Horn Hasan, our graphic designer Jodie Penn, and our trainers—AmondaRose Igoe, Jennifer Connell, Kathy Sipple, and Linda Albright as well as the many other women who have contributed their guidance, expertise, love and support. We're grateful to each of you.

Rev. Robin V. Schwoyer who wrote the foreword for this book. You hold the spirit of an angel and the wisdom of a sage. We cherish your friendship, easy presence, and humor, and we know that your words will reach deep into the hearts of our readers.

We are forever grateful to our friends and families who lovingly support our inspirations, projects, and unconventional ways of being—with your guidance and love we remain steadfast in our vision for life.

Above all, we are grateful to the Universal Spirit and to life itself for providing opportunities for continued growth and mindful living!

With much love and deep gratitude,
Sue Urda and Kathy Fyler

About Rev. Robin V. Schwoyer

Robin V. Schwoyer, the founder of HeARTs Wellness®, Inc and Pink HeARTs Wellness, is an ordained Minister in the Episcopal Church as well as a Holistic wellness practitioner. She is a certified teacher of various healing modalities, an Inspirational/motivational speaker, published author and a Yoga instructor. Robin has used the creative arts with youth, families and clients in outreaches for over 20 years. The power to open the heart and heal the mind & body through holistic care and the Arts has always fascinated her.

Several women in her family died at early ages due to cancer, stress and heart related diseases. Robin's interest in pastoral care started early in childhood as she watched the effects on her loved ones and the family.

Robin's mother, Shirley, blessed her daughters with her inquisitive spiritual nature and very creative talents. As Shirley lived with the challenges of cancer, she taught her daughters key lessons on the important qualities of life.

Today, Pink HeARTs Wellness for Women is a tribute to Shirley and the many women like her. It is the collaboration of many persons who desire to help women live life to the fullest wherever they are in their journey.

Through the perspective of love, we connect our hearts seeking to be filled from the sacred well of life.

Contact Robin through her website:
www.PinkHeartsWellness.com

About Sue Urda and Kathy Fyler

Sue and Kathy have been friends for 25 years and business partners since 1994. They have received awards and accolades for their businesses over the years and they love their latest venture into book publishing where they've helped more than 150 women achieve their dreams of becoming published authors and reaching #1 on Amazon's Bestseller list.

Their pride and joy is Powerful You! Inc., which they claim is a gift from Spirit. They love traveling the country producing meetings and tour events to gather women for business, personal and spiritual growth. Their greatest pleasure comes through connecting with the many inspiring and extraordinary women who are a part of their network.

The strength of their partnership lies in their deep respect, love and understanding of one another, and their complementary skills and knowledge. Kathy is a technology enthusiast and free-thinker. Sue is an author, speaker and thought-leader with a love of creative undertakings. Their respect, appreciation and love for each other are boundless.

Together their energies combine to feed the flames of countless women who are seeking truth, empowerment, joy, peace and connection with themselves, their own spirits and other women.

Reach Sue and Kathy:
Powerful You! Inc.
973-248-1262
info@powerfulyou.com
www.powerfulyou.com

Powerful You! Women's Network
Networking with a Heart

OUR MISSION is to empower women to find their inner wisdom, follow their passion and live rich, authentic lives.

Our Vision
Powerful You! Women's Network is founded upon the belief that women are powerful creators, passionate and compassionate leaders, and the heart and backbone of our world's businesses, homes, and communities.

Our Network welcomes all women from all walks of life. We recognize that diversity in our relationships creates opportunities.

Powerful You! creates and facilitates venues for women who desire to develop connections that will assist in growing their businesses. We aid in the creation of lasting personal relationships and provide insights and tools for women who seek balance, grace and ease in all facets of life.

Our Beliefs

❖We believe in the power of connections.
❖We believe in the power of being present.
❖We believe in the power of relationships.
❖We believe in the power of women.

We believe in the power of devoted groups of collaborative and grateful individuals coming together for the purpose of personal growth and
assisting others in business and in life.

We believe in a Powerful You!

More About
Powerful You! Women's Network

Powerful You! was founded in January 2005 to gather and connect women for business, personal and spiritual growth.

Our monthly chapter meetings provide a collaborative and comfortable space for networking, connections and creating personal relationships. Meetings include introductions, discussion topic, speaker presentation, growth and success share, mini-mastermind, and a gratitude share.

Member Benefits *(Some available to non-members too!)*

- Powerful You! Learning Center
- Powerful You! Virtual Network Meetings
- Online Social Networking Website
- Special Advertising with Powerful You!
- Discounts on Meetings and Events
- Speak at Powerful You! Meetings

For more information about Powerful You! visit our website.

www.powerfulyou.com

Follow us online:
Twitter: @powerfulyou
Facebook: www.facebook.com/powerfulyou

Join or Start a Chapter for
Business, Personal & Spiritual Growth

Would You Like to Contribute to Our Next Anthology Book?

Become an Author Easily, Effortlessly and Soon!

Do you have a story in you? Most people do.

If you've always wanted to be an author, and you can see yourself partnering with other women to share your story, or if you have found yourself daunted by the prospect of writing a whole book on your own, an anthology book may be your answer.

We are committed to helping women express their voices. Learn more at:

Powerful You! PUBLISHING
Sharing Wisdom ~ Shining Light

Powerful You! Publishing
973-248-1262
powerfulyoupublishing.com

Live Consciously Now!

CPSIA information can be obtained at www.ICGtesting.com
Printed in the USA
LVOW04s0738210115

423651LV00003B/14/P